Contents

Section Three — Grammar

Section Four — In the Exam

Published by CGP

From original material by Richard Parsons

Editors:
David Broadbent
Rachel Grocott
Lucy Loveluck
Anthony Muller
Holly Poynton
Sabrina Robinson
Jo Sharrock
Rebecca Tate

With thanks to Glenn Rogers and Nicola Woodfin for the proofreading.

ISBN: 978 1 84762 147 4

www.cgpbooks.co.uk
Printed by Elanders Ltd, Newcastle upon Tyne.
Clipart from Corel®

Introduction to SPaG

Sadly, this kind of SPaG has nothing to do with pasta, but it is pretty important at GCSE — not just for bagging those important extra marks, but for making your written work make sense.

SPaG stands for Spelling, Punctuation and Grammar

1) SPaG marks are given for correct spelling, punctuation and grammar in certain GCSE subjects.

2) The subjects that award separate SPaG marks are:

- English Literature
- History
- Geography
- Religious Studies

3) 5% of the total marks for these GCSE subjects will be given for SPaG.

4) Even if a subject doesn't award marks for SPaG, it's still really important to be able to use spelling, punctuation and grammar correctly.

Read the question Carefully

You won't be tested on SPaG for every question, so you need to read the exam paper carefully. Questions with SPaG marks will be clearly marked, like this:

> **2** Explore how prejudice affects the characters in *Of Mice and Men*. Use evidence to back up your answer.
>
> **[40]**
>
> **(Total for spelling, punctuation and grammar = 6 marks)**
> **(Total for Question 2 = 46 marks)**

This shows how many SPaG marks are available for this question.

SPaG Marks are Really Important

1) 5% doesn't sound like many marks, but it could make a whole grade's difference.

2) You'll throw away easy marks if you make silly spelling mistakes or forget how to use punctuation and grammar properly.

3) Remember though, even if your SPaG is perfect, if an examiner can't read your handwriting, it could still cost you marks.

SPaG — it sounds more exciting than it actually is...

Now that you know what SPaG marks are, you need to make sure that your spelling, punctuation and grammar skills are completely up to scratch. That's why this book will come in handy.

Plurals

When you have two or more of something, you need to change the noun to the plural form.

Most Words Add '-s' to make the Plural

Usually nouns just add '-s' on the <u>end</u> to make them <u>plural</u>.

human ⟹ human<u>s</u>   place ⟹ place<u>s</u> ⟸ '-<u>s</u>' is added to the noun to make it <u>plural</u>.

Some words need '-es'

1) Add '-<u>es</u>' to nouns ending in a <u>hissing sound</u> — '<u>s</u>', '<u>ch</u>', '<u>sh</u>', '<u>x</u>' and '<u>z</u>'.
2) You <u>can't</u> just add '-s' to these nouns because they'd be <u>difficult to say</u>. You need to add '-<u>es</u>' to help you <u>pronounce</u> the word.

glass + '-<u>s</u>' = glass<u>s</u> ✘ ⟹ glass + '-<u>es</u>' = glass<u>es</u> ✔

watch + '-<u>s</u>' = watch<u>s</u> ✘ ⟹ watch + '-<u>es</u>' = watch<u>es</u> ✔

bush + '-<u>s</u>' = bush<u>s</u> ✘ ⟹ bush + '-<u>es</u>' = bush<u>es</u> ✔

box + '-<u>s</u>' = box<u>s</u> ✘ ⟹ box + '-<u>es</u>' = box<u>es</u> ✔

waltz + '-<u>s</u>' = waltz<u>s</u> ✘ ⟹ waltz + '-<u>es</u>' = waltz<u>es</u> ✔

There are Two Plural Forms for words that End in '-y'

1) Look at the letter <u>in front</u> of the '<u>y</u>'.
2) If it's a <u>vowel</u> — the letters 'a', 'e', 'i', 'o' or 'u' — just <u>add</u> '-<u>s</u>'.

ke<u>y</u> ⟹ keys   pla<u>y</u> ⟹ play<u>s</u> ⟸ The letter before the '<u>y</u>' is '<u>a</u>' — a <u>vowel</u>, so you only need to add an '-<u>s</u>'.

3) If the letter <u>in front</u> of the '<u>y</u>' is a <u>consonant</u> — <u>drop</u> the '<u>y</u>' and add '-<u>ies</u>'.

part<u>y</u> ⟹ part<u>ies</u>   fl<u>y</u> ⟹ fl<u>ies</u> ⟸ The letter before the '<u>y</u>' is '<u>l</u>' — a <u>consonant</u>. You need to <u>drop</u> the '<u>y</u>' and add '-<u>ies</u>'.

Plurals aren't just about sticking 's' on the end...

Make sure you learn the rules for these plural words. One way to check the plural of words which end in 's', 'ch', 'sh', 'x' and 'z' is to say them aloud — if they end in a hissing sound, they need an '-es' ending.

Plurals

Most **Plurals** of **Names** just need an '**-s**' on the end

You <u>always</u> add an '-<u>s</u>' when you write the plural of a name (unless the name <u>ends</u> with '-s').

Both Henr<u>ys</u> were good at horse riding.

Even though the <u>letter before</u> 'y' is 'r', a <u>consonant</u>, because it's a name you just add an '-<u>s</u>'.

There were four James<u>es</u> who became King.

This name <u>ends</u> with '<u>s</u>', so it follows the '-<u>es</u>' rule on page 2 — if a word ends in '-s', add '-<u>es</u>' for the <u>plural</u>.

Words that **End** in '**o**' can be **Tricky**

1) Words that end in '<u>o</u>' <u>usually</u> add '-<u>s</u>' to make their plural, e.g. piano<u>s</u>, disco<u>s</u>.

2) Some words ending in 'o' are <u>different</u> though — they take '-<u>es</u>' instead:

potato + '-<u>s</u>' = potato<u>s</u> ✘ ⟹ potato + '-<u>es</u>' = potato<u>es</u> ✔

tomato + '-<u>s</u>' = tomato<u>s</u> ✘ ⟹ tomato + '-<u>es</u>' = tomato<u>es</u> ✔

hero + '-<u>s</u>' = hero<u>s</u> ✘ ⟹ hero + '-<u>es</u>' = hero<u>es</u> ✔

echo + '-<u>s</u>' = echo<u>s</u> ✘ ⟹ echo + '-<u>es</u>' = echo<u>es</u> ✔

volcano + '-<u>s</u>' = volcano<u>s</u> ✘ ⟹ volcano + '-<u>es</u>' = volcano<u>es</u> ✔

3) Unfortunately, there's <u>no pattern</u> to this rule — you just have to <u>remember</u> the <u>exceptions</u>.

Most words **Ending** in '**f**' and '**fe**' add '**-ves**' to make the **Plural**

1) For these words you need to <u>change</u> the '<u>f</u>' into a '<u>v</u>', and add '-<u>es</u>'.

loa<u>f</u> ⟹ loa<u>ves</u>   shel<u>f</u> ⟹ shel<u>ves</u>

li<u>fe</u> ⟹ li<u>ves</u>   wi<u>fe</u> ⟹ wi<u>ves</u>

2) But there are <u>awkward ones</u> that <u>keep</u> the '<u>f</u>' and just add '-<u>s</u>'.

chie<u>fs</u>   belie<u>fs</u>   proo<u>fs</u>   ree<u>fs</u>   che<u>fs</u>

There are always exceptions to learn...

There's no getting around it — you've got to learn the exceptions to the rules. Make a list of some tricky plurals and use it to test yourself. It won't take long before you know them off by heart.

Plurals

Some plurals are irregular and don't follow any rules — look out for these common tricksters...

Other words have Irregular Plurals

1) Some words <u>don't</u> follow a <u>pattern</u> for making their plurals.
2) Instead of <u>adding</u> or <u>removing</u> letters you might have to <u>change</u> the spelling of the <u>original word</u>.
3) These words change their <u>vowel sound</u> when they become plural:

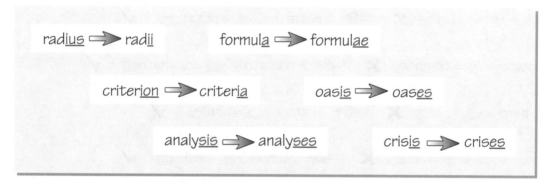

wom<u>a</u>n ⇒ wom<u>e</u>n   t<u>oo</u>th ⇒ t<u>ee</u>th

f<u>oo</u>t ⇒ f<u>ee</u>t   m<u>ou</u>se ⇒ m<u>i</u>ce

4) Some words that come from <u>other languages</u> also have <u>irregular plurals</u>:

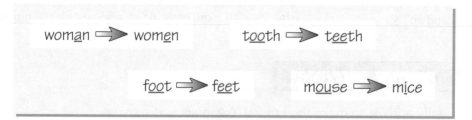

rad<u>ius</u> ⇒ rad<u>ii</u>   formul<u>a</u> ⇒ formul<u>ae</u>

criter<u>ion</u> ⇒ criter<u>ia</u>   oas<u>is</u> ⇒ oas<u>es</u>

anal<u>ysis</u> ⇒ anal<u>yses</u>   cris<u>is</u> ⇒ cris<u>es</u>

Some words Stay the Same in the Plural

Some words don't change at all — they're the <u>same</u> in both <u>singular</u> and <u>plural forms</u>:

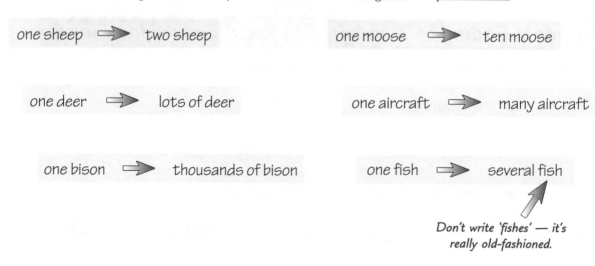

one sheep ⇒ two sheep   one moose ⇒ ten moose

one deer ⇒ lots of deer   one aircraft ⇒ many aircraft

one bison ⇒ thousands of bison   one fish ⇒ several fish

Don't write 'fishes' — it's really old-fashioned.

Not all words are different in the plural form...

It might make your life a little easier, having words that don't change at all in the plural form. All you need to do is remember which words they are. A good place to start is by learning the list above.

Suffixes and Prefixes

You add suffixes and prefixes to a word to change its meaning. Prefixes go at the beginning of a word, and suffixes go at the end.

Prefixes and *Suffixes* are used to make *New Words*

Prefixes and suffixes are <u>letters</u> that don't make any sense by themselves, but when they're <u>added</u> to <u>other words</u>, they <u>change</u> the word's <u>meaning</u>:

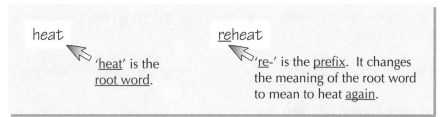

heat

'<u>heat</u>' is the <u>root word</u>.

reheat

'<u>re-</u>' is the <u>prefix</u>. It changes the meaning of the root word to mean to heat <u>again</u>.

Remember — 'pre' means 'before', so prefixes go at the start of words.

garden

'<u>garden</u>' is the <u>root word</u>.

gardener

'<u>-er</u>' is the <u>suffix</u>. It changes the meaning of the root word to mean <u>someone who works</u> in a <u>garden</u>.

Look out for these **Common Prefix Spelling Errors**

1) The <u>spelling</u> of the root word <u>never changes</u> when a <u>prefix</u> is added.
2) Don't fall into the trap of <u>adding</u> or <u>taking away</u> letters:

Sometimes you need to add a hyphen between the prefix and the word (see p.43).

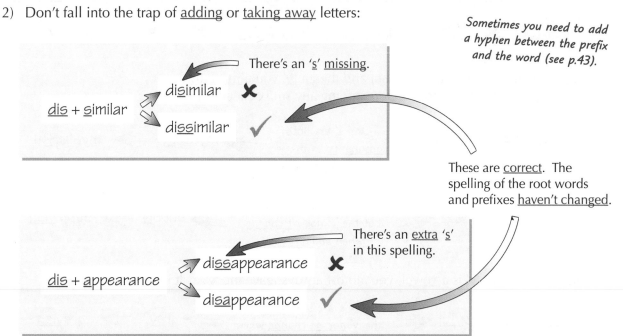

<u>dis</u> + <u>s</u>imilar

di<u>s</u>imilar ✘   There's an '<u>s</u>' missing.

di<u>ss</u>imilar ✔

These are <u>correct</u>. The spelling of the root words and prefixes <u>haven't changed</u>.

<u>dis</u> + <u>a</u>ppearance

di<u>ss</u>appearance ✘   There's an <u>extra</u> '<u>s</u>' in this spelling.

di<u>sa</u>ppearance ✔

It's simple — don't touch the root word when you add a prefix...

Spelling words with prefixes isn't too hard because you don't need to add or take away any letters. All you need to do is learn how to spell the root word... and how to spell the prefix. Easy peasy.

Suffixes and Prefixes

If only it was all so easy. Suffixes come with some pesky rules that you need to know.

Learn these Rules for words ending in 'e'

1) If the <u>root word ends</u> in '<u>-e</u>' and the first letter of the suffix is a <u>vowel</u>, you need to <u>drop</u> the 'e'.

achie<u>ve</u> + <u>-able</u> ⇨ achiev<u>able</u>   car<u>e</u> + -er ⇨ car<u>er</u>

2) If there is a <u>soft</u> 'g' or '<u>c</u>' just before the '<u>-e</u>' in the <u>root word</u>, you <u>don't drop</u> the '<u>e</u>' (unless the suffix starts with an '<u>e</u>' or '<u>i</u>').

knowled<u>ge</u> + -able ⇨ knowled<u>geable</u>   coura<u>ge</u>+ -ous ⇨ coura<u>geous</u>

3) If the first letter of the suffix is a <u>consonant</u>, <u>keep</u> the 'e'.

lo<u>ve</u> + -ly ⇨ lov<u>ely</u>   car<u>e</u> + -less ⇨ car<u>eless</u>

4) There are some <u>exceptions</u> to this rule:

arg<u>ue</u> + -<u>ment</u> ⇨ arg<u>ument</u>   horrible + -ly ⇨ horri<u>bly</u>

There are a Few more Rules you need to know

1) Make sure you spell the suffix '<u>-ful</u>' with only <u>one</u> 'l' — e.g. beautiful, not beautifull.

2) The suffixes '<u>-tion</u>', '<u>-sion</u>' and '<u>-cian</u>' all sound like '<u>-shun</u>'. Make sure you've got the <u>right one</u>.

poli<u>tition</u> ✘ ⇨ poli<u>tician</u> ✓   revolu<u>sion</u> ✘ ⇨ revolu<u>tion</u> ✓

3) If a <u>root word ends</u> with a consonant and then a '<u>y</u>' you <u>almost always</u> have to <u>change</u> the '<u>y</u>' to an '<u>i</u>' before adding any suffix except '<u>-ing</u>'.

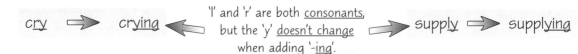

earl<u>y</u> ⇨ earl<u>ier</u> ⟵ 'l' and 'r' are both <u>consonants</u>, so the 'y' ⟶ myster<u>y</u> ⇨ myster<u>ious</u>
changes when adding '<u>-ous</u>'.

cr<u>y</u> ⇨ cr<u>ying</u> ⟵ 'l' and 'r' are both <u>consonants</u>, but the 'y' <u>doesn't change</u> when adding '<u>-ing</u>'. ⟶ suppl<u>y</u> ⇨ suppl<u>ying</u>

4) If the letter before 'y' is a <u>vowel</u>, you almost always <u>leave</u> the 'y' as it is.

jo<u>y</u> ⇨ jo<u>yful</u> ⟵ 'o' and 'e' are both <u>vowels</u>, so the 'y' <u>doesn't change</u> when adding a <u>suffix</u>. ⟶ gre<u>y</u> ⇨ gre<u>yish</u>

Make sure you've learnt these rules...

It's important that you learn the rules on this page because those tricky suffixes often mean letters have to be changed in the root word. You'll need to learn the exceptions to the rules as well.

Suffixes and Prefixes

To help you work out how to spell words with suffixes on the end you can use the C-V-C rule.

The **C-V-C Rule** tells you when to **Double Letters**

1) If you are adding a <u>suffix</u> that begins with a <u>vowel</u>, you can use the <u>C-V-C rule</u>.

2) For most words, if the last three letters go <u>consonant - vowel - consonant (C-V-C)</u>...

re<u>gret</u>   be<u>gin</u>   up<u>set</u>   for<u>got</u>   All these words end with <u>C-V-C</u>.

3) ...you <u>double</u> the <u>last letter</u> when you add the suffix.

regret+ -<u>ing</u> ⇨ regre<u>t</u>ting   '-<u>ing</u>' starts with a vowel, so double the '<u>t</u>'.

There are some exceptions — the letters 'c', 'h', 'q', 'w', 'x' and 'y' are rarely (or never) doubled when a suffix is added.

forgot+ -<u>en</u> ⇨ forgo<u>t</u>ten   '-<u>en</u>' starts with a vowel, so double the '<u>t</u>'.

The **C-V-C Rule** doesn't **Always Work**

1) You can only use the <u>C-V-C</u> rule on a word if its last <u>syllable</u> is <u>stressed</u>.
The <u>stressed syllable</u> is the syllable which is <u>emphasised</u> when you say the word.

<u>PHO</u>tograph   pho<u>TOG</u>raphy   photo<u>GRAPH</u>ic   This example shows how the <u>stressed syllable</u> can <u>move</u> in similar words.

You can tell if you're stressing the <u>wrong syllable</u> because it usually <u>sounds strange</u>.

2) If the <u>first letter</u> of the suffix <u>isn't a vowel</u>, you <u>don't</u> need to double the last letter:

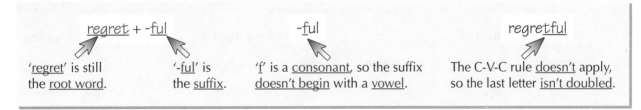

<u>regret</u> + -<u>ful</u>   -<u>ful</u>   regret<u>ful</u>

'regret' is still the <u>root word</u>.   '-<u>ful</u>' is the <u>suffix</u>.   'f' is a <u>consonant</u>, so the suffix <u>doesn't begin</u> with a <u>vowel</u>.   The C-V-C rule <u>doesn't</u> apply, so the last letter <u>isn't doubled</u>.

3) When you <u>add a suffix</u> to a <u>root word</u>, do a <u>quick check</u> to see if you can use the C-V-C rule:

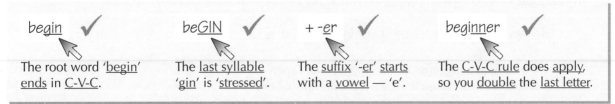

be<u>gin</u> ✓   be<u>GIN</u> ✓   + -<u>er</u> ✓   begi<u>n</u>ner ✓

The root word '<u>begin</u>' <u>ends</u> in <u>C-V-C</u>.   The <u>last syllable</u> '<u>gin</u>' is '<u>stressed</u>'.   The <u>suffix</u> '-<u>er</u>' starts with a <u>vowel</u> — 'e'.   The <u>C-V-C rule</u> does <u>apply</u>, so you <u>double</u> the <u>last letter</u>.

Don't forget those double letters...
The next time you're not sure whether to double a letter, check those stressed syllables and think C-V-C.
The rule is quite hard to learn and you'll need to spend a bit of time practising it before it'll sink in.

Silent Letters and Unstressed Vowels

Silent letters and unstressed vowels — you can't hear them, but they're there... These nasty little things could cause you more trouble than a breadless sandwich if you're not careful, so pay attention.

Some words have *Silent Letters*

1) Silent letters are <u>letters</u> which you <u>don't hear</u>.

2) Words with silent letters are <u>tricky</u> to spell because you <u>can't hear</u> all the letters when you say the word. This means you might <u>miss letters out</u> if you're not careful.

3) Make sure you <u>learn</u> the <u>correct spellings</u> of <u>common words</u> with silent letters for your exam — it's an <u>obvious mistake</u> for the examiner to notice.

Learn the *Correct Spelling* of these words

1) Here are some <u>common examples</u> of words with <u>silent letters</u> — loads more have them, but these are the <u>main ones</u>:

Words with a **silent 'h'**

which	whether	when
while	chemist	white

Words with a **silent 'b'**

lamb	womb	debt
tomb	subtle	doubt

Words with a **silent 'w'**

write	whole	wrong
two	answer	who

Words with a **silent 'k'**

kneel	knife	knight
knot	know	knowledge

Words with a **silent 'c'**

scene	science	conscience
scent	disciple	descend

Words with a **silent 't'**

listen	Christmas
castle	tsar

Words with a **silent 'l'**

half	could
would	should

2) The <u>context</u> of a sentence might give you <u>clues</u> about how to spell some words.

Medieval knights wore multiple layers of armour.

This should be '<u>knight</u>' in this <u>context</u> — it's spelt with a silent '<u>k</u>' when it means a 'medieval soldier'.

Practise spelling the words you're not sure about...

They're silent, but they're deadly... If you miss letters out, you'll be throwing spelling marks away. Learn this page carefully — it might help to write out the correct spelling of each word three times.

Silent Letters and Unstressed Vowels

Words with **Double Letters** can be **Tricky**

1) Words with <u>double letters</u> are hard to spell because you say <u>double letters</u> as a <u>single sound</u>.

2) This means that the <u>second</u> (doubled) <u>letter</u> is like a <u>silent letter</u> because you <u>can't hear it</u>.

3) The only thing you can do to <u>remember</u> how to <u>spell</u> these words is to <u>learn them</u>:

a<u>cc</u>o<u>mm</u>odation	a<u>ss</u>ociation	emba<u>rr</u>a<u>ss</u>
add<u>re</u>ss	di<u>ff</u>erent	e<u>ss</u>ential
a<u>pp</u>a<u>ll</u>ing	disa<u>pp</u>ear	eventua<u>ll</u>y

exa<u>gg</u>erate	jewe<u>ll</u>ery	po<u>ss</u>e<u>ss</u>
i<u>mm</u>ediately	nece<u>ss</u>ary	su<u>cc</u>eed
i<u>rr</u>esistible	o<u>cc</u>asion	su<u>cc</u>e<u>ss</u>

See p.24-25 for more on mnemonics.

4) Using <u>mnemonics</u> can help you to remember how to spell tricky words.

a<u>cc</u>o<u>mm</u>odation <u>2</u> <u>c</u>ots need <u>2</u> <u>m</u>attresses in any a<u>cc</u>o<u>mm</u>odation.

Unstressed Vowels can cause **Misspellings**

1) Sometimes the <u>vowel sound</u> in a word isn't <u>clear</u> — these sounds are called <u>unstressed vowels</u>.

2) Spelling these words can be <u>awkward</u> because the vowels don't make the sound you would <u>expect</u>.

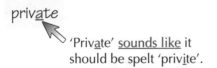

priv<u>a</u>te
'Private' <u>sounds like</u> it should be spelt 'priv<u>ite</u>'.

sep<u>a</u>rate
'Separate' <u>sounds like</u> it should be spelt 'sep<u>e</u>rate'.

3) Unfortunately there isn't a rule for spelling words with <u>unstressed vowels</u> — you'll just have to <u>learn</u> how to spell them. Here are some useful examples:

defin<u>i</u>tely	interfer<u>e</u>nce	govern<u>m</u>ent	d<u>e</u>scribe
r<u>i</u>diculous	diff<u>e</u>rence	gen<u>e</u>ral	comp<u>a</u>ny

---

Don't get stressed about unstressed vowels...

Misspelling words with unstressed vowels is something that people do all the time, so you'll look really good if you learn how to spell the most common ones correctly. It'll be worth it in the end.

i Before e Rule

This page is about the 'i before e' rule, and its exceptions. It's a confusing rule, but if you learn it you'll be able to write sentences like, "Scientists believe the thief seized eight of his neighbour's glaciers."

The *'i' before 'e'* rule

1) The letters '<u>i</u>' and '<u>e</u>' often <u>appear together</u>, so it's easy to <u>confuse</u> which way round they should be.

2) Use the '<u>i' before 'e' rule</u> to help you <u>remember</u> how to spell words where 'i' and 'e' <u>appear together</u>.

'<u>i</u>' <u>before</u> '<u>e</u>' <u>except after</u> '<u>c</u>', but only when it <u>rhymes</u> with <u>bee</u>.   The <u>whole word</u> doesn't need to <u>rhyme</u> with <u>bee</u>, just the '<u>ie</u>' sound.

3) These are some <u>examples</u> that you should <u>learn</u>:

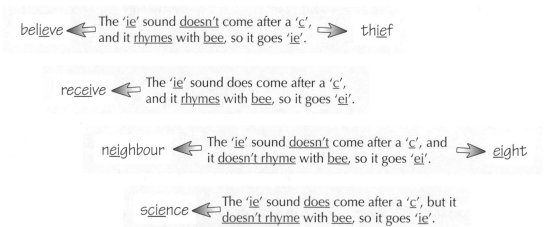

bel<u>ie</u>ve ⟵ The '<u>ie</u>' sound <u>doesn't</u> come after a '<u>c</u>', and it <u>rhymes</u> with <u>bee</u>, so it goes '<u>ie</u>'. ⟹ th<u>ie</u>f

rec<u>ei</u>ve ⟵ The '<u>ie</u>' sound does come after a '<u>c</u>', and it <u>rhymes</u> with <u>bee</u>, so it goes '<u>ei</u>'.

n<u>ei</u>ghbour ⟵ The '<u>ie</u>' sound <u>doesn't</u> come after a '<u>c</u>', and it <u>doesn't rhyme</u> with <u>bee</u>, so it goes '<u>ei</u>'. ⟹ <u>ei</u>ght

s<u>ci</u>ence ⟵ The '<u>ie</u>' sound <u>does</u> come after a '<u>c</u>', but it <u>doesn't rhyme</u> with <u>bee</u>, so it goes '<u>ie</u>'.

Learn the Exceptions to the Rule

Not all words with an '<u>ie</u>' sound follow this rule — there are a <u>few exceptions</u> you need to <u>learn</u>:

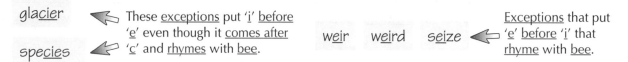

gla<u>cie</u>r ⟵ These <u>exceptions</u> put '<u>i</u>' <u>before</u> '<u>e</u>' even though it <u>comes after</u> '<u>c</u>' and <u>rhymes</u> with <u>bee</u>.

spe<u>cie</u>s

w<u>ei</u>r   w<u>ei</u>rd   s<u>ei</u>ze ⟵ Exceptions that put '<u>e</u>' <u>before</u> '<u>i</u>' that <u>rhyme</u> with <u>bee</u>.

Words with a **Prefix** or a **Suffix** can **Break** the **Rule**

1) Adding a <u>prefix</u> or <u>suffix</u> to a word will sometimes <u>break</u> the '<u>i before e</u>' <u>rule</u>:

queue ⟹ queu<u>ei</u>ng   fancy ⟹ fan<u>cie</u>d

icy ⟹ ic<u>ie</u>st   insure ⟹ r<u>ei</u>nsure

2) Just remember that <u>prefixes</u> and <u>suffixes</u> have their <u>own spelling rules</u> (see p.5-7), and they take <u>priority</u> over the 'i before e' rule.

Don't forget that you just need to look at the 'ie' sound...

The 'ie' rule can be difficult if you don't check all the parts of the rule carefully. There's also a bunch of exceptions that don't help either. You know what to do though — learn them, learn them, learn them.

Forming Comparatives

Comparing one thing to another will be useful in your essays, but forming comparatives incorrectly leads to all sorts of problems. So read these pages carefully and learn how to do it properly.

Adding '-er' and 'than' can form a Comparative

For <u>short words</u> like 'tall', 'short', 'happy' and 'big', take the <u>adjective</u> and add the <u>suffix</u> '-<u>er</u>' to the <u>end</u>, followed by '<u>than</u>'.

For more on suffix spelling rules see pages 5-7.

An adjective describes a noun.

big + -er ⇨ bigger ⇨ Asia is <u>bigger than</u> Europe.

To make the adjective '<u>big</u>' a comparative, you add the suffix '-<u>er</u>'.

The <u>C-V-C rule</u> means you need to <u>double</u> the letter 'g' in the adjective '<u>big</u>'.

Finally, add '<u>than</u>' to complete the <u>comparison</u>.

happy + -er ⇨ happier ⇨ Jacob is <u>happier than</u> Esau.

Add the suffix '-<u>er</u>' to the adjective '<u>happy</u>'.

'happy' ends in a <u>consonant</u> and a '<u>y</u>', so you need to change the '<u>y</u>' to an '<u>i</u>' when adding the suffix.

Add '<u>than</u>' to complete the comparison.

Use 'more' and 'than' to compare Longer Words

1) When you're comparing <u>longer words</u> you don't need to add '-<u>er</u>'.

2) If you want to say the <u>first</u> thing is <u>better</u> or <u>bigger</u> than the <u>second</u> you use '<u>more</u>' and '<u>than</u>':

Steinbeck is <u>more</u> popular <u>than</u> Salinger. ✓   Steinbeck is <u>popularer</u> than Salinger. ✗

'more' goes <u>in front</u> of the adjective 'popular'.

'than' goes <u>after</u> the <u>adjective</u>.

Adding '-<u>er</u>' to the adjective gives you a word that <u>doesn't exist</u>.

3) If you want to say the <u>first</u> thing <u>isn't as good</u> you use '<u>less</u>' instead of '<u>more</u>':

Steinbeck is <u>less</u> popular <u>than</u> Salinger.   Ethiopia is <u>less</u> developed <u>than</u> Kenya.

Put '<u>less</u>' in front of the adjective instead of '<u>more</u>'.

You still need to remember to add '<u>than</u>' or it <u>won't make sense</u>.

4) If you want to say two things are <u>the same</u>, you replace both words with '<u>as</u>' instead:

Steinbeck is <u>as</u> popular <u>as</u> Salinger.   Shanghai is <u>as</u> expensive <u>as</u> Paris.

Put '<u>as</u>' <u>before</u> and <u>after</u> the adjective.

Comparatives are quite straightforward...

Just don't forget to add 'than' before the second thing you're comparing when you're using 'more' or 'less' to compare two things. Without 'than' you might not even be writing a proper sentence.

Forming Comparatives

A few more bits and bobs on comparatives to get your head around.

Learn these Common Forms for Best and Worst

1) Sometimes comparing things isn't <u>enough</u> — you need to say which is the <u>best</u> or <u>worst</u>. Learn these <u>common forms</u>.

You <u>don't</u> need to do <u>anything</u> to the words in the left-hand box.

'The Crucible' is <u>good</u>.

Adjective	Comparative	Superlative
good	better	best
bad	worse	worst
much / many	more	most
little	less	least
few	fewer	fewest

The words in the right-hand box are <u>superlatives</u>, which are '<u>most</u>' words — you don't need any other comparative words, but you need to use '<u>the</u>'.

'The Crucible' is <u>the best</u>.

With the words in the middle box you need to put '<u>than</u>' after them, otherwise the sentence <u>won't make any sense</u>.

'The Crucible' is <u>better than</u> '1984'.

2) Be careful <u>not to confuse</u> comparatives and superlatives — you <u>can't</u> say things like '<u>more better</u>' or '<u>worst than</u>'.

You can use '-est' to say something is the Most

1) One way of saying something has the <u>most</u> of a <u>characteristic</u> is to put '<u>-est</u>' on the <u>end</u> of an adjective.

You can only use this method for short adjectives.

2) You should treat '<u>-est</u>' just like any other <u>suffix</u> — it follows the same <u>spelling rules</u> (see p.6-7).

Those are the grey<u>est</u> clouds.

'Greyest' means '<u>the most grey</u>'. The 'y' <u>stays the same</u> because the letter <u>before</u> the 'y' is a <u>vowel</u> — 'e'.

The heav<u>iest</u> rainfall is inland.

'Heaviest' means the '<u>most heavy</u>'. The '<u>y</u>' in 'heavy' <u>changes</u> to 'i' as you are adding a <u>suffix</u> that <u>isn't</u> '-ing'.

Ralph is the brav<u>est</u> boy on the island.

Because the <u>root word</u> 'brave' ends in '<u>e</u>' and the first letter of the <u>suffix</u> is a <u>vowel</u>, you <u>drop</u> the '<u>e</u>' when you add '-est'.

'-est' follows the same rules as other suffixes...

I bet you thought you were done with suffixes, but they just creep back in. Remember, if you're saying something is the best or the most, then you need to use 'the' — otherwise you won't make sense.

Forming Comparatives

Superlatives for *Longer Words* need '*Most*'

1) <u>Longer words</u> (three syllables or more) don't <u>sound right</u> if you add '<u>-est</u>'.
2) You need to use '<u>most</u>' instead.

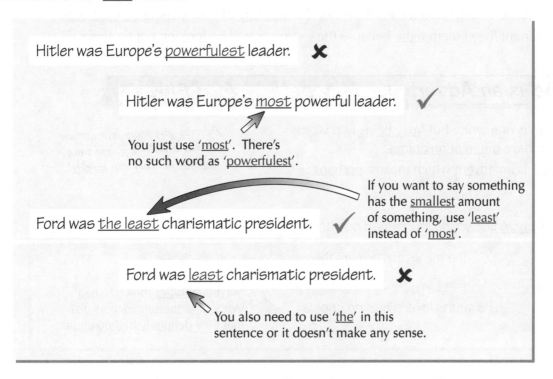

Hitler was Europe's <u>powerfulest</u> leader. ✗

Hitler was Europe's <u>most</u> powerful leader. ✓

You just use '<u>most</u>'. There's
no such word as '<u>powerfulest</u>'.

If you want to say something
has the <u>smallest</u> amount
of something, use '<u>least</u>'
instead of '<u>most</u>'.

Ford was <u>the least</u> charismatic president. ✓

Ford was <u>least</u> charismatic president. ✗

You also need to use '<u>the</u>' in this
sentence or it doesn't make any sense.

Never use '*Most*' and '*-est*' *Together*

You can either use '<u>most</u>' or add '<u>-est</u>' on the <u>end</u> of your <u>adjective</u> — don't use them <u>both together</u>.

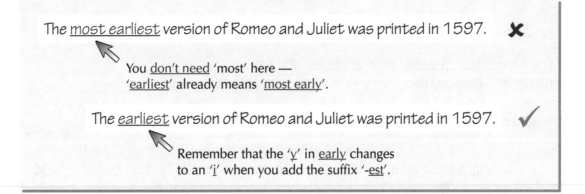

The <u>most earliest</u> version of Romeo and Juliet was printed in 1597. ✗

You <u>don't need</u> 'most' here —
'<u>earliest</u>' already means '<u>most early</u>'.

The <u>earliest</u> version of Romeo and Juliet was printed in 1597. ✓

Remember that the '<u>y</u>' in <u>early</u> changes
to an '<u>i</u>' when you add the suffix '<u>-est</u>'.

You have to choose between 'most' and '-est'...

To be the best you've got to use comparatives and superlatives like the best. That means avoiding silly mistakes that might pop up if you're not careful. 'Most' and '-est' are enemies, so keep them apart.

Commonly Misused Words

These pages are about the words you love to hate — the ones that sound similar but mean different things.

It's **Easy** to **Misuse** certain words

1) Words which <u>sound</u> the <u>same</u> but have <u>different meanings</u> can be <u>misused</u> in exams.

2) If you use the wrong word it can also make the <u>meaning</u> of your writing <u>very unclear</u>.

3) It's important to get them <u>right</u>, because the examiner will be <u>looking out</u> for them.

'**Maybe**' is an **Adverb** but '**May be**' is a **Verb Phrase**

1) '<u>Maybe</u>' is one word, but '<u>may be</u>' is two words — they have <u>different meanings</u>.

2) '<u>Maybe</u>' is an <u>adverb</u> which means '<u>perhaps</u>':

Adverbs give more information about a verb. E.g. 'He sang <u>quietly</u>' or 'They ran <u>quickly</u>'.

<u>May</u>be the young lovers had no choice.

This means that <u>perhaps</u> the young lovers had no choice.

The young lovers had no choice.   Maybe <u>modifies</u> the verb '<u>had</u>'. Without it, the sentence means that they <u>definitely</u> had no choice.

3) '<u>May be</u>' is a <u>verb phrase</u> — it means that something is only a <u>possibility</u>:

Both of the sentences below mean <u>similar things</u>, but they have to be <u>phrased</u> and <u>structured differently</u>:

Charles I <u>may be</u> the least popular monarch in English history.

<u>Maybe</u> Charles I is the least popular monarch in English history.

If you can <u>replace</u> '<u>may be</u>' with '<u>might be</u>' and the sentence still <u>makes sense</u>, then you're using the <u>right one</u>.

Charles I <u>might be</u> the least popular monarch in English history. ✓

<u>Might be</u> Charles I is the least popular monarch in English history. ✗

 This <u>doesn't make sense</u>, so it should be '<u>maybe</u>' instead of '<u>may be</u>'.

'*Maybe*' and '*may be*' mean different things...

The easiest way to sort out your 'maybes' from your 'may bes' is to use 'might be'. It's all very straightforward — if 'might be' fits in the sentence, then you should use 'may be', not 'maybe'. Phew!

Commonly Misused Words

'Anyway' and 'Anybody' are both One Word

1) 'Anyway' is an adverb which means 'regardless' — it's spelt as one word.

2) 'Any way' means 'any method' — it's spelt as two separate words.

It was a difficult exam, but I did well anyway. ← The exam was hard, but I did well regardless.

This question is asking if there is any method that would allow him to work tomorrow. → Is there any way he can work tomorrow?

3) 'Everybody' is a pronoun which means 'every person' — it's spelt as one word. 'Every body' means 'every group' or 'every physical body' — it's spelt as two separate words.

Do you know where everybody is? ← This question is asking where all the people are.

Every body of power has to make rules.   Every body needs minerals and vitamins.

In this context 'every body' means 'every group'.   In this context 'every body' means 'every physical body'.

4) The same idea applies to 'anybody' and 'any body'. 'Anybody' means 'any person', 'any body' means 'any group' or 'any physical body'.

'No one' is Two Words but 'Nobody' is One Word

1) You must write 'no one' as two words. Don't write 'noone'.

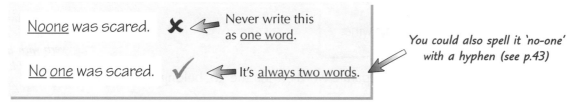

Noone was scared. ✗ ← Never write this as one word.

No one was scared. ✓ ← It's always two words.

You could also spell it 'no-one' with a hyphen (see p.43)

2) 'Nobody' is always one word.

No body was scared. ✗   Nobody was scared. ✓

Never write this as two words.   It's always one word.

3) Other words for talking about people are one word too. E.g. 'everyone', 'someone' and 'anyone'.

4) Words ending in '-thing' and '-where' are also all one word. E.g. 'everything' and 'nowhere'.

Don't break up one word into two words...

You can accidentally change the meaning of a sentence by breaking up a single word into two. The last thing you want is for your writing to be confusing, so be careful not to make these mistakes.

Commonly Misused Words

Make sure you learn the differences between these words. Plenty of practice is a good start.

'Always' and 'Altogether' are Adverbs

1) 'Always' and 'altogether' are spelt as one word. Don't confuse them with 'all ways' and 'all together'.

2) 'Always' means 'at all times', but 'all ways' means 'every way' or the 'total number of methods':

Atticus always fights for justice.

Atticus fights for justice at every opportunity.

All ways out of the city are blocked.

Every way (or route) is blocked.

3) 'Altogether' means 'completely' or 'in total'. 'All together'
means 'at the same time', 'in the same place' or 'in a group':

I have nine albums altogether. ← This is the number of albums in total.

Let's jump all together. ← This means 'let's jump all at the same time'.

I am altogether exhausted.

This means 'completely exhausted'.

'Into' is a Preposition or Part of a Verb

A preposition is a word which tells you how things are related, e.g. 'in', 'above' or 'before'.

1) 'Into' is a preposition which shows that something is moving towards the inside of something.

The boy ran into the house. ← This example shows the direction of the boy. If you can replace 'into' with the word 'inside' and it still makes sense, you're using it correctly.

2) 'Into' is also part of the verb 'to turn into'.

He turned the water into wine.

An infinitive verb is the most basic form of a verb with the word 'to' in front of it, e.g. 'to see'.

3) 'In' and 'to' are spelt as two separate words when the 'to' belongs to a verb.

They came in to look around. ← 'to' belongs to the verb 'look'. It's part of an infinitive verb. If you replace 'in' with 'inside', you still need the word 'to'.

4) 'In' and 'to' can be spelt as two separate words when the 'to' is a preposition.

This sentence means she gave her homework to her teacher. → She turned her homework in to her teacher.

If you used 'into' by mistake, the sentence would mean something completely different — that the homework was transformed into her teacher.

Write quickly but carefully in exams...

It's tempting to rush your writing when you're in an exam, but that's how commonly misused words can sneak in. When you rush your writing you can make mistakes you wouldn't normally make.

Commonly Misused Words

'A lot' is **Always** written as **Two Words**

A common mistake to make is writing 'alot' instead of 'a lot' — 'alot' is never correct.

There are alot of reasons. ✗ ← Never write this as one word.

There are a lot of reasons. ✓

Practise is a **Verb** but Practice is a **Noun**

1) Practise is a doing word, which means it's a verb — it's spelt with an 's'.

The boys practise hunting.   She is practising the piano.

2) Practice is something you go to, so it's a noun — it's spelt with a 'c'.

The boys have hunting practice.   Tennis practice is hard work.

You can use this mnemonic to help you remember:

Practise is a verb (like is).   Practice is a noun (like ice).

See p.24-25 for more on mnemonics.

It's the **Same** as Advise and Advice, or Devise and Device

With advise/advice and devise/device it's easier to remember which is the noun and which is the verb because they sound different.

He asked Mr Birling to advise him.   Mr Birling's advice was useless.

Use 's' for a verb   Use 'c' for a noun

The Germans devised the Schlieffen Plan.   The Americans built a nuclear device.

Practise Practise Practise Practice makes perfect...

'Practise' and 'practice' always cause trouble. They're two of the hardest words to get right in the whole English language. Remember, 'practice' is a thing, an event or an idea. 'Practise' is a verb. Job done.

Commonly Misused Words

More of the same on these pages, I'm afraid. It turns out a lot of words get mixed up.

Licence and License are like Practice and Practise

1) License is a verb — it's spelt with an 's'.

> Some restaurants are licensed to sell alcohol.

> Doctors have had to be licensed for hundreds of years.

2) Licence is a noun — it's spelt with a 'c'.

> Some provisional licences were converted to full driving licences without a test.

> They have a licence to sell their product internationally.

Don't confuse Passed with Past

1) Passed with '-ed' is an action — it has to be done by someone or something.

> Wolsey passed many laws.

This means Wolsey approved lots of laws — Wolsey did the passing.

> The Israelites passed through the Red Sea.

This means the Israelites went through the Red Sea.

2) Past with a '-t' is not an action — it's a description.

The word 'past' can be used to describe a period of time...

> The play is set in the past.

> The Inspector uncovers the family's past.

... or it can describe where something went.

> The children run past Boo Radley's house.

> The Gulf Stream goes past Florida.

This use of 'past' is easily confused with 'passed'. To check you've used the right one, look at the word before 'past' — if it's a verb 'past' is normally correct, if it's a noun (or pronoun) then it's probably 'passed'.

Don't let 'em fool you just because they sound the same...

Examiners know these are common mistakes and will be quick to take off marks if they see you making them. Don't let them catch you out — think to yourself: 's' = verb, 'c' = noun, 's' = verb, 'c' = noun...

Commonly Misused Words

Affect is the Action but Effect is the Result

Affect is an action which influences something, but an effect is the result of an action.

> Drinking too much alcohol affects your liver. ⟵ Drinking alcohol is doing something to your liver.

> Too much alcohol has an effect on your liver. ⟵ This is talking about the result of drinking too much alcohol.

Accept is Totally Different to Except

1) Accept is a verb — it means to 'agree' with something or to 'receive' something.

> Most scholars accept that a man named Jesus existed. ⟵ This means that scholars agree that a man called Jesus existed.

> The victims accepted compensation. ⟵ This means that the victims received compensation.

2) Except means 'not including'.

> This means that only Ralph didn't turn to savagery. ⟶ Everyone turns to savagery except Ralph.

Where, Were and Wear

These three words sound similar, but they have very different meanings.

1) Where is used for places and positions.   Where is Mumbai?

2) Wear is what you do with clothes, shoes and jewellery.   I wear my costume.

3) Were is the past form of are.   They were studying glaciers.

> If you're not sure about 'were' in a sentence, use 'are' instead.
> If it still makes sense then 'were' is probably right.

Don't confuse these words — it'll affect your marks...

Some more commonly misused words to get on top of. One of the hardest ones to pin down is 'affect' and 'effect', so put some practice in to make sure you get it right. That'll impress the examiner.

Commonly Misused Words

The English language is crammed full of homophones — words that sound the same but are spelt differently and mean different things. So there's still plenty more to learn, I'm afraid...

There, Their and They're

1) There goes with where — it's about places and positions.

> There is evidence to support this.
>
> There aren't any glaciers there.

2) Their means it belongs to them.

> Their sacred text is the Qur'an.
>
> Their argument is based on misleading facts.

3) They're is short for 'they are'.

> They're still researching climate change.
>
> 'They're' is too informal for exams — use 'they are' instead.

'Your' and 'you're' follow a similar pattern — 'your' means it belongs to you, 'you're' is short for 'you are'.

Hear and Here

1) 'Here' is the opposite of 'there'.

> Come here.   Here they come.   I'm not here.

2) 'Hear' is when you listen.

> Hear the music.   Dogs can hear everything.   Can you hear it?

3) If you're still confused, you can use these mnemonics to help you remember:

> There's an 'ear' in hear.   Here goes with there.

See p.24-25 for more on mnemonics.

Similar words with different meanings don't make things any easier...

These words can be confusing, but it's really important that you learn the difference between them so you can use them properly. Otherwise your writing will confuse the examiner like nobody's business.

Commonly Misused Words

To / Too / Two — they're All Different

This one's a really common mistake, so make sure you don't slip up:

1) To means 'towards' or is part of a verb.

They're going to Geneva. ← 'to' means 'in the direction of'.

He wants to reform. ← 'to' is part of the verb 'to reform'.

2) Two is just the number '2'.

Two million pounds ← It might help to think of 'tw' for 'twice'.

3) Too means 'too much' or 'also'.

This novel's too long... ← This means that the novel is overly long.

... and it's boring too. ← This means that it is also boring.

Off means 'Away From' or 'Not On' — the rest of the time use Of

Off usually means 'away from' or 'not on'. Of is just a linking word:

This means 35% taken away from the price. → All items 35% off

The lights were off. ← This means the lights were 'not on'.

Snowball is full of ideas. ← 'of' links the words together. → A man of morals

Our is a Pronoun and Are is a Verb

1) 'Our' is a possessive pronoun (see p.58).
2) 'Are' is a present tense form of the verb 'to be' (see p.65).

It is our decision. ← 'our' means that the decision 'belongs' to them.

We are deciding. ← 'are' tells you what the subject of the sentence is doing.

Sometimes, it's too easy to get words muddled...

The difference between to, two and too isn't very difficult to learn, but it's one of the most common mistakes that people make. If you use this page you should get the hang of it without too much trouble.

Commonly Misused Words

Unfortunately there are still plenty more words that sound the same but are spelt differently.

Watch out for **Though**, **Thought**, **Through** and **Thorough**

These words <u>look similar</u>, so it's easy to write the <u>wrong one</u> by <u>mistake</u>, but it could <u>cost you</u> if you do.

Electric cars are a good idea, <u>though</u> they have their drawbacks. ⟵ 'Though' means '<u>however</u>'.

I <u>thought</u> about the exam. ⟵ '<u>Thought</u>' is the <u>past tense</u> of the verb '<u>to think</u>'...

I had a <u>thought</u>. ⟵ ... or '<u>a thought</u>' can be '<u>an idea</u>'.

'<u>Through</u>' means 'going from one side of something to the other'. ⟹ It went <u>through</u> the window.

He was <u>thorough</u> in his work. ⟵ '<u>Thorough</u>' means '<u>careful</u>' or '<u>in depth</u>'.

Don't mix up **Piece** and **Peace**...

1) '<u>Piece</u>' means '<u>part of</u>'.
2) '<u>Peace</u>' is the opposite of war — it means '<u>calm</u>'.

It's a <u>piece</u> of cake. ⟵ '<u>piece</u>' means a '<u>part of</u>' the cake here.

After the war the two sides agreed a <u>peace</u> treaty. ⟵ Here '<u>peace</u>' means '<u>an end to war</u>'.

...or **Whether** and **Weather**

1) '<u>Whether</u>' means '<u>if</u>'.
2) '<u>Weather</u>' means '<u>atmospheric conditions</u>' — rain, sun, cloud etc.

An agnostic is someone who doesn't know <u>whether</u> there's a god.

↖ You could swap '<u>whether</u>' for '<u>if</u>'.

The <u>weather</u> in rainforests is hot and rainy.

↖ Only use '<u>weather</u>' when you're talking about the <u>climate</u>.

We're almost through these commonly misused words...

Hmm, it's worth being thorough and putting a bit of thought into learning these words, even though there are a lot of them. On a brighter note, there aren't a lot of pages on commonly misused words left.

Commonly Misused Words

It's easy to confuse 'Buy', 'By' and 'Bye'

1) 'Buy' is what you do when you <u>pay for something</u>.

> George and Lenny want to <u>buy</u> a farm. ⇐ 'buy' means '<u>to purchase</u>' here.

2) 'Bye' is a shortening of '<u>goodbye</u>'.

> The men shouted, "<u>Bye</u>, lads!" ⇐ In this sentence 'Bye' means '<u>goodbye</u>'.

3) 'By' is a <u>linking word</u>. It usually means 'beside' or 'due to'.

> Coastal landforms are caused <u>by</u> erosion. ⇐ Here the coastal landforms are made '<u>due to</u>' erosion.

Don't use 'Them' when you Mean 'Those'

For more on pronouns see p.57-59.

1) '<u>Them</u>' is a pronoun — <u>never</u> use it with the <u>noun</u> it <u>replaces</u>.
2) '<u>Those</u>' is used to <u>point out</u> specific things.

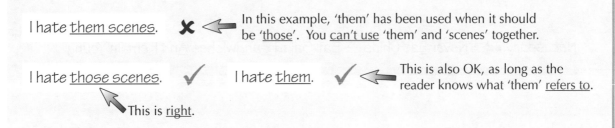

I hate <u>them scenes</u>. ✗ ⇐ In this example, 'them' has been used when it should be '<u>those</u>'. You <u>can't use</u> 'them' and 'scenes' together.

I hate <u>those scenes</u>. ✓   I hate <u>them</u>. ✓ ⇐ This is also OK, as long as the reader knows what 'them' <u>refers to</u>.

This is <u>right</u>.

Teach and Learn are Opposites

<u>Teaching</u> means '<u>giving out knowledge</u>', and <u>learning</u> means '<u>taking in knowledge</u>'.

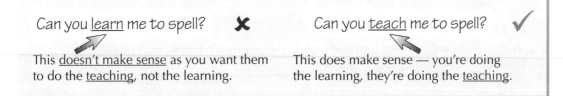

Can you <u>learn</u> me to spell? ✗   Can you <u>teach</u> me to spell? ✓

This <u>doesn't make sense</u> as you want them to do the <u>teaching</u>, not the learning.   This does make sense — you're doing the learning, they're doing the <u>teaching</u>.

At last, the end of all the misused words — hurrah!

Phew, that was a slog. Now you've got to the end you need to make sure you can remember all this stuff. Use these pages to write sentences that use each of the commonly misused words correctly.

Spelling Tricky Words

No matter how hard you practise, there will always be some words that you struggle to spell correctly. Spelling mistakes are really obvious to the examiner, so use these tips to help you spell perfectly.

Use these Spelling Tips

1) Keep a <u>list</u> of the words that you find <u>tricky</u>.
   <u>Practise</u> spelling them until you get them right <u>every time</u>.

2) Use <u>flashcards</u> and write the spelling on the front, and put the <u>meaning</u> on the <u>back</u>. That way you can <u>test</u> the <u>spelling</u> as well as the <u>meaning</u>.

3) <u>Learn spelling rules</u> — the '<u>i before e</u>' rule and the <u>C-V-C rule</u> can help you work out how a word is spelt.

Make up Mnemonics

1) Try using <u>mnemonics</u> — these are <u>sentences</u> or <u>phrases</u> that can <u>help</u> you <u>remember</u> spellings.

2) <u>Make up</u> your <u>own mnemonics</u> for words that you find tricky.

3) The <u>first letters</u> of these phrases help you remember how to spell difficult words:

Rhythm ➡ <u>R</u>hythm <u>H</u>as <u>Y</u>our <u>T</u>wo <u>H</u>ips <u>M</u>oving

Necessary ➡ <u>N</u>ever <u>E</u>at <u>C</u>hips — <u>E</u>at <u>S</u>alad <u>S</u>andwiches <u>A</u>nd <u>R</u>emain <u>Y</u>oung

Because ➡ <u>B</u>ig <u>E</u>lephants <u>C</u>an <u>A</u>lways <u>U</u>nderstand <u>S</u>mall <u>E</u>lephants

Tight, light, sight, fight ➡ First letters (e.g. 't', 'l', 's' and 'f'), then <u>I</u>'ve <u>G</u>ot <u>H</u>airy <u>T</u>ights

Could, would, should ➡ First letters (e.g. 'c', 'w' and 'sh'), then <u>O</u>h <u>U</u> <u>L</u>ittle <u>D</u>arling

---

You need a mnemonic to spell mnemonic...

<u>M</u>onsters <u>N</u>ever <u>E</u>at <u>M</u>onkeys <u>O</u>r <u>N</u>ewts <u>I</u>n <u>C</u>afés. It doesn't matter what technique you use, as long as it gets results. Silly sentences seem to stick in your head best, so be as ridiculous as you like.

Spelling Tricky Words

You can use *Other Special Rules* for *Tricky Words*

When you make up your own rules for <u>unusual spellings</u>, you don't have to just use the first letters of the words in a sentence. You can also create other <u>made-up rules</u> to give you a good chance of <u>remembering</u> tricky words in the <u>exam</u>. Here are a few to get you going:

1) *Funny Sentences* can *Remind* you of spellings you keep forgetting

These sentences help you remember the <u>bits</u> in the words that are <u>often misspelt</u>.

There's <u>a rat</u> in sep<u>arat</u>e.　　There's a <u>lie</u> in bel<u>ie</u>f.　　The <u>secret</u>ary has a <u>secret</u>.

<u>Remember</u> these smaller words and you'll find it much <u>easier</u> to spell the longer words.

You <u>gain</u> when you get a bar<u>gain</u>.　　Emma faced a dil<u>emma</u>.

2) You can make *Special Rules* for *Difficult Spellings*

These rules help you remember which <u>letters</u> are <u>single</u> and which are <u>doubled</u>.

Ne<u>c</u>e<u>ss</u>ary — a vicar has <u>1</u> <u>c</u>ollar and <u>2</u> <u>s</u>ocks.

Emba<u>rr</u>a<u>ss</u> — <u>2</u> <u>r</u>osy cheeks and <u>2</u> <u>s</u>carlet cheeks.

Try making up your <u>own rules</u> like these for words with <u>double letters</u> that you find tricky to spell.

3) *Rules* for words which *Sound* the *Same* are *Really Useful*

These rules help you remember which <u>similar-sounding word</u> is which.

Station<u>ery</u> is for things like pencils and pap<u>er</u>.
Station<u>ary</u> is for things that aren't moving, like a p<u>ar</u>ked c<u>ar</u>.

Compl<u>e</u>ment adds something to make it <u>e</u>nough.
Compl<u>i</u>ment puts you in the l<u>im</u>elight.

De<u>ss</u>erts have 2 <u>s</u>ugar<u>s</u>.
De<u>s</u>erts just have <u>s</u>and.

Funny sentences can help you remember all sorts of things...

These funny sentences are pretty darn handy. You could make a list of all the words you find hard to spell and then make up rhymes or mnemonics to help you remember every single one of them.

Spelling Tricky Words

It can be hard to think about spelling when you're in the middle of an exam. This page has plenty of helpful hints which could help you prepare. They really are marvellous, so read on my friend, read on.

Spell Sensibly in the Exam

Even if you've <u>prepared properly</u>, there's still a chance that your mind might go <u>blank</u> in the exam. The important thing is <u>not to panic</u> — remember this <u>simple advice</u> to help you get those SPaG marks:

1) If you're <u>quoting</u> from <u>source material</u> in the exam, <u>check</u> your spelling against the extract. The examiner won't be impressed if you <u>misspell</u> a word that you've been <u>given</u>.

2) If you're <u>struggling</u> to spell a word — <u>sound it out</u> in your head. Work out how <u>each syllable</u> sounds and have a <u>sensible go</u> at spelling it.

3) <u>Write out</u> any troublesome words in <u>rough</u>, to see whether they <u>look right</u> before you use them in your essay.

4) If you're still <u>not sure</u> how to spell a word, try to use a <u>different word</u> that <u>means the same</u>, that you definitely <u>know</u> how to spell.

5) Even if you're <u>not sure</u> whether you've spelt a word correctly, <u>stick</u> to the spelling you've chosen. It's more obvious to the examiner that you've made a mistake if you spell the <u>same word</u> three <u>different ways</u>.

6) If you notice a <u>mistake</u>, put a <u>neat line</u> through the word and <u>rewrite</u> it clearly above.

7) Leave <u>5 minutes</u> at the <u>end</u> of the exam to <u>check</u> your work.

See p.89-91 for more on correcting mistakes.

Learn these Common Exam Words

Some words come up in <u>essays</u> time and time again, so make sure you get them <u>learnt</u>.

analyse	criticism	interesting	separately
argument	definitely	opinion	strengths
basically	exaggerate	probably	successful
because	experience	recommend	weaknesses
believe	independent	reference	whether

If you're not sure which words you struggle with, have a look through some old homework to see which mistakes your teacher keeps correcting.

Don't panic in the exam — just remember all these helpful tips...

These words are the kinds of things that sound really good in essays, but only if you spell them correctly. If you learn them all now, you'll be all set for writing a beautifully spelt essay in your exam.

Misspelt History Words

These pages contain some tricky words that you might need in your exam. They're just a starting point though — make sure you make your own vocab lists for the subjects you're taking.

History uses fairly Uncommon words

Only learn the words that you'll need for the subjects you're taking.

You might have heard some of these words in everyday usage, but some of them seem to be stuck in the pages of History textbooks. You need to know what they mean, as well as how to spell them:

anaesthetics — drugs which numb the body so that no pain is felt

antibiotics — medicine which kills bacteria

artillery — large guns used in warfare, particularly for bombardment

assassination — the murder of an important person, often for political reasons

biased — when a source has been affected by the author's opinion

democracy — a system of government where people elect representatives to political office

fascism — the political idea that a country should be led by one person — a dictator

government — the people who hold political office and who govern a country

hyperinflation — when money inflates at a very fast rate, and loses a lot of its value

parliament — an institution where the elected government meets to debate and pass laws

propaganda — information that is usually biased, used to promote a particular group

reliability — how reliable a source might be

reparations — payments made by one country to another to pay for damage caused by war

suffrage — the right to vote in elections (suffragettes are women who promote this right)

surgery — when a doctor operates on a patient

There are some awkward words in history...

Crikey — more words to learn. Unfortunately these are just a starting point. There are loads more hard-to-spell words in History that aren't here — you've still got to learn them or you may lose marks.

Misspelt Geography Words

This page is important if you're doing GCSE Geography. If you're not, you can probably skip it...

Geography uses lots of Technical Terms

Some of these words are very specific to Geography, so if you've not learnt them you might struggle:

businesses — more than one commercial company or business

cyclone — a storm with a circular wind pattern

debt — when money or goods are owed

desert — a large, dry, barren area of land

development — the improvement, advancement or progression of something

drought — a long period of below average rainfall

environment — the natural world around us

erosion — the process where something is gradually worn away

eutrophication — when fertilisers pollute rivers, lakes or seas

hydraulic — when liquid moves in a confined space, under intense pressure

indigenous — a person or thing that originates from a certain region or country

refugee — someone who leaves their home because of war or persecution

trade bloc — when a group of countries reduce trade barriers between them

vegetation — the collection of plants found in a particular area

volcano — a rupture in the Earth's crust that allows lava and hot gas to escape

All good geographers can spell 'volcano' correctly...

Geographers really like using long words, and as you can see, some of them are pretty hard to spell. That's why you need to learn them. Use the classic 'look, cover, write, check' and you'll be set.

Misspelt English Words

English examiners are experts on spelling, so you've got to make sure you get it right in your exam.

You'll need these words in English Essays

Most of these words are technical terms that you'll need to talk about types of writing:

alliteration — when consonants are repeated at the beginnings of nearby words

assonance — when words share the same vowel sound, but the consonants are different

empathy — when someone understands what someone else is experiencing and feeling

enjambment — when a sentence runs from one line of poetry onto the next one without pausing

figurative — something that isn't meant to be taken literally

foreshadowing — where the reader is given clues about what will happen later

genre — the type of literature a piece is, e.g. romantic, gothic

imagery — descriptive language that creates a picture for the reader

irony — when the author says one thing but means the opposite

metaphor — a way of describing something by saying that it is something else

onomatopoeia — when a word sounds like what it means, e.g. fizz, buzz and crash

personification — when you talk about something non-human as if it's a person

playwright — somebody who writes plays

rhythm — a pattern of sounds created by stressed and unstressed vowels

simile — a way of describing something by saying that it is like something else

Spelling is key to a good SPaG mark...

SPaG and English go hand in hand — just like good spelling and top SPaG marks. Make sure you learn these words properly — then you can whip them out in the exam and impress the examiner.

Misspelt Religious Studies Words

RS is not easy, and spelling the words correctly is half the battle. That's where this page comes in handy.

Religious Studies has a lot of Long Words

RS has some of the trickiest words of the bunch — make sure you've got them covered.

agnosticism — a belief that it's impossible to know whether or not there's a god

atheism — a complete denial of the existence of a god

benevolence — a tendency to act kindly or charitably

bereavement — the loss of someone close to you through their death

conscience — an inner feeling of what's right and wrong

disciple — a follower or student of the beliefs of another person

euthanasia — ending someone's life to relieve their suffering, especially from a terminal illness

immortality — the belief that the soul will live on after the death of the body

omnipotence — having unlimited power so that all things are possible

omniscience — knowing everything (in the past, the present and the future)

pacifism — the idea that war and physical violence are wrong under all circumstances

prejudice — judging something or someone with no good reason

reincarnation — the idea that a soul is reborn in a new body after death

resurrection — being brought back to life after death (either by body or by soul)

surrogacy — when a woman bears a child for another woman

You know the drill by now...

Well, I don't know about you, but I'm pretty tired of spelling now. At least this is the last page, although that doesn't mean you can slack off. Get these RS words learnt, just like the rest.

Practice Questions

These practice questions are on all the stuff from this section. If there's anything you're not sure about, go back to the page about it and make sure you've got it learnt before you move on to the exam practice.

Practice Questions

1) Rewrite these nouns to make them plural.

   a) *class*   d) *tooth*   g) *volcano*   j) *belief*

   b) *city*   e) *church*   h) *life*   k) *deer*

   c) *child*   f) *claw*   i) *disco*   l) *lady*

2) Add the prefixes in brackets to each of the words below.
   Make sure you check any double letters.

   a) *(in) numerable*   c) *(un) necessary*   e) *(un) timely*   g) *(sub) marine*

   b) *(dis) approve*   d) *(pro) creation*   f) *(im) maturity*   h) *(ir) relevant*

3) Using the C-V-C rule, add the suffixes in brackets to the words below.
   Be sure to check your spelling.

   a) *success (ful)*   c) *thought (less)*   e) *budget (ed)*   g) *begin (er)*

   b) *forget (ing)*   d) *conquer (ed)*   f) *forgot (en)*   h) *follow (ed)*

4) Write out the correct spelling in each of the examples below.

   a) *goverment / government*   e) *species / speceis*   i) *sutle / subtle*

   b) *det / debt*   f) *could / coud*   j) *deity / diety*

   c) *believe / beleive*   g) *wen / when*   k) *seperately / separately*

   d) *assended / ascended*   h) *atheists / athiests* l) *sceintific / scientific*

5) Correct each of the sentences below so that the comparatives make sense and are spelt correctly.

   a) 'Romeo and Juliet' is <u>most</u> popular than 'Macbeth' in schools, maybe because the story is <u>more good</u>.

   b) In Geography, the <u>bestest</u> way to get a <u>betterer</u> mark than my friends is to do the <u>more</u> studying.

   c) China has the <u>most largest</u> population in the world, with <u>most</u> than 1.3 billion people.

   d) Morale was very important in the trenches — <u>more happier</u> soldiers meant <u>more effectiver</u> offensives.

Practice Questions

6) Rewrite these sentences using the correct underlined word or words so that they make most sense.

   a) I <u>may be</u>/<u>maybe</u> able to help, but then again <u>may be</u>/<u>maybe</u> not.

   b) Is there <u>anyway</u>/<u>any way</u> to drill <u>in to</u>/<u>into</u> the depths of the deepest glaciers?

   c) I was <u>all together</u>/<u>altogether</u> confused by her attempt to turn a rabbit <u>into</u>/<u>in to</u> a dove.

   d) They came <u>into</u>/<u>in to</u> investigate <u>every body's</u>/<u>everybody's</u> alibis.

7) Rewrite these sentences using the correctly spelt underlined word.

   a) <u>They're</u>/<u>Their</u> aim was to avoid the impact of war, but it still had an <u>affect</u>/<u>effect</u> on the country.

   b) In the <u>passed</u>/<u>past</u>, Jews <u>where</u>/<u>were</u> discouraged from marrying someone from another religious faith.

   c) The Inspector is a plot <u>device</u>/<u>devise</u> designed to force the Birlings to <u>accept</u>/<u>except</u> their wrongdoings.

   d) It is important to <u>practice</u>/<u>practise</u> emergency drills in countries <u>wear</u>/<u>where</u> earthquakes are common.

8) Rewrite these sentences, using the correctly spelt underlined words in each one.

   a) It was <u>though</u>/<u>thought</u> that $30 billion was lost within <u>two</u>/<u>too</u> days as a result of the Wall Street Crash.

   b) The values in 'To Kill a Mockingbird' will <u>learn</u>/<u>teach</u> you a lot because many of <u>them</u>/<u>those</u> are still relevant.

   c) <u>Our</u>/<u>Are</u> research into renewable energy has been very <u>through</u>/<u>thorough</u> in the last few years.

   d) The teachings <u>off</u>/<u>of</u> Judaism and Islam are against euthanasia. Catholics are opposed <u>two</u>/<u>to</u> it <u>too</u>/<u>to</u>.

9) Write down a mnemonic or silly rule to help you remember how to spell each of these difficult words.

   a) *strength*   e) *probably*   i) *separately*

   b) *exaggerate*   f) *recommend*   j) *successful*

   c) *basically*   g) *reference*   k) *criticism*

   d) *analyse*   h) *definitely*   l) *interesting*

Exam Practice

Practice Questions

10) Check each word for spelling mistakes. If any words are spelt incorrectly, rewrite them with the correct spelling.

a) *mispelt*   e) *cieling*   i) *insightful*

b) *shelfs*   f) *alphabetical*   j) *brushs*

c) *suppossed*   g) *acept*   k) *criticism*

d) *progressing* h) *sieze*   l) *allthough*

You might have got to the end of the practice questions, but there's more fun to be had. Have a go at these exam-style questions.

Exam Practice

1) There are 6 spelling mistakes in the passage below. Using a pen, circle the errors and write any corrections above — give yourself 1 minute. The first one has been done for you.

opportunity

During World War I, many women had the (oportunity) to work for the first time. Men's jobs were suddenly availible because they were away fighting, and women were happy to take them. They wanted to prove that they where just as capable as men. Women worked as bus conductors and farm workers, and took tecnical jobs in engineering workshops. The women who worked in factories made esential goods for the war, like weapons an uniforms, which had a direct effect on the war effort.

2) There are 6 spelling mistakes in the passage below. Using a pen, circle the errors and write any corrections above — give yourself 1 minute. The first one has been done for you.

In the UK, people are living longer because of advances in medicine and improved

standards

living (standerds) This means that the proportion of older people in the population is rising. To cope with this, the goverment is gradualy increasing the retirement age to 68 for everyone by 2046. This means alot more people will be paying taxes for longer. They are also encouraging women to go back to work after having children by giving them extra tax credits for childcare. These strategies maybe working, but it is still to early to tell.

Exam Practice

3) There are 6 spelling mistakes in the passage below. Using a pen, circle the errors and write any corrections above — give yourself 1 minute. The first one has been done for you.

Abortion is when a foetus is removed from the womb before it is able to survive. Many

believers

religious ⟨beleivers⟩ think that abortion is always wrong. They believe that all life belongs

to God and is theirfore holy. Only God can choose when it starts or ends. Some religious

believers think that alowing a woman to choose weather or not to have an abortion is a way

off showing compassion. This is especialy true if the mother was raped, is very young, or the

child will have serious health problems.

4) There are 6 spelling mistakes in the passage below. Using a pen, circle the errors and write any corrections above — give yourself 1 minute. The first one has been done for you.

structure

The ⟨stucture⟩ of 'Of Mice and Men' is circuler. The novel begins and ends with

George and Lennie in the same woodland clearing. On both ocassions, Lennie has

done something wrong and the two freinds have been forced to run away. This leaves

the reader with the inpression that the events of the novel were inevitable and the

characters were helples to do anything to change them.

5) There are 6 spelling mistakes in the passage below. Using a pen, circle the errors and write any corrections above — give yourself 1 minute. The first one has been done for you.

led

Mikhail Gorbachev brought in reforms that ⟨lead⟩ to major changes in the USSR.

Gorbachev's abandonning of the Brezhnev Doctrine was vital in bringing about the

end of the Berlin Wall. The Brezhnev Doctrine was the guarantee that the USSR woud

all ways get involved if socialism was threatened elsewhere. Scraping the doctrine

made it possible for Eastern European countries to escape from USSR interferance.

Capital Letters

Using capital letters seems obvious, but there's more to them than you think. Don't throw away valuable marks by skipping this page because you think you know it — I promise it's useful.

Use Capitals at the Start of Sentences

Make sure that your capital letters are obvious — they should be twice as big as normal letters.

Every sentence <u>starts</u> with a <u>capital letter</u>.

The novel is about racism. It was set in the 1930s, but I think it's still relevant. ✓

<u>Both</u> of these sentences <u>need</u> capital letters at the <u>beginning</u>.

'<u>I</u>' has a <u>capital letter</u> <u>wherever</u> you use it.

Some words Always start with a Capital Letter

Some words start with a capital letter, even in the <u>middle of a sentence</u>:

1) <u>People's names</u> and <u>titles</u>   Tsar Nicholas II was unpopular.   John Proctor faced a choice.

2) Names of <u>organisations</u>   Royal Geographical Society   Church of England

3) Titles of <u>books</u> and <u>plays</u>   Animal Farm   Lord of the Flies

<u>Short words</u> like 'of', 'the' and 'upon' <u>don't</u> have <u>capital letters</u>.

4) <u>Towns</u> and names of <u>places</u>   Sheffield   Kingston upon Thames, London

5) <u>Countries</u>, <u>nationalities</u> and <u>languages</u>   I am French. I come from France and I speak French.

6) <u>Religions</u>, the <u>names of gods</u> and <u>religious believers</u>   Islam is a religion. Muslims worship Allah.

7) Names of <u>days</u> and <u>months</u>   Wednesday   January   February

<u>Names</u> for <u>particular people</u>, <u>places</u> and <u>things</u> are called '<u>proper nouns</u>'.

8) <u>Public holidays</u> and <u>religious days</u>   Christmas   Diwali   Easter

Capitalising some words can be Tricky

Some nouns are capitalised <u>sometimes</u>, but <u>not</u> at other times.

 Some kings wear crowns.

 The King wore his crown.

If you're talking about kings in <u>general</u>, you <u>don't</u> need a <u>capital letter</u>.

If you're talking about <u>a particular king</u>, you need a <u>capital letter</u>.

London is a capital city with a capital 'L'...

Yes, this all seems very simple, but you still need to make sure you know when to add a capital letter to the beginning of words. If you don't use them properly, you could end up looking a bit silly...

Ending Sentences

Use punctuation to finish sentences correctly — you'll be throwing marks away if you don't.

Full Stops End sentences

1) Full stops are used to end statements.

2) If you're writing an essay, you'll finish most of your sentences with a full stop.

The children portray Boo Radley as a monster. This reflects the adults' prejudices. ✓

This is correct — each sentence finishes with a full stop.

Question Marks show the end of a Question

1) Question marks show that you're asking a question:

Why were the 1930s a time of famine?

2) Some sentences tell you about a question but don't actually ask one.

Ralph asks Jack why he hates him.

This isn't actually asking a question, so there's no question mark. It's a statement about what Ralph does — it just needs a full stop.

Exclamation Marks show Strong Emotions

1) Exclamation marks are used to show strong emotions, or to emphasise something.

2) You shouldn't need to use exclamation marks in your essays, unless you're quoting a line which uses one.

The sheep continue to chant, "Four legs good, two legs better!"

3) If you use exclamation marks in your writing, never use more than one to end a sentence.

What a surprise!!! ✗   What a surprise! ✓

Don't use exclamation marks too often — they'll lose their impact.

Use exclamations and questions correctly to get the marks...

In the exam, you'll mainly use full stops, but that doesn't mean you don't have to learn about exclamation and question marks. Using a full stop when you need a question mark is a big no-no.

Commas

Without commas, lists would be a jumbled-up mess, and long sentences wouldn't make much sense.

Commas Separate items in a List

1) A list that doesn't contain commas is really <u>hard to understand</u>:

   Floods damage houses farms roads and bridges.

2) Add a comma after <u>each item</u> to make your list clear.

3) Put '<u>and</u>' or '<u>or</u>' between the last two items in the list. Remember,
   you <u>don't</u> need to use a comma before the final '<u>and</u>' or '<u>or</u>'.

   Floods damage houses, farms, roads and bridges. ✓   You only need to use commas
   in lists of <u>three or more</u> items.

4) Use commas to <u>separate</u> two <u>adjectives</u> next to each other which could be separated by '<u>and</u>'.

   He was a cruel, ruthless king.   It was a light green jumper.

   You <u>could</u> put 'and' here,   You <u>couldn't</u> put 'and' here,
   so you <u>need a comma</u>.   so you <u>don't need a comma</u>.

A Comma combines Two Points

1) Two sentences can be joined using a <u>connective</u>, and sometimes with a <u>comma</u> as well.

2) The most common
   <u>short connectives</u> are:

   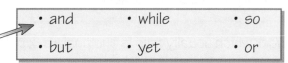

• and	• while	• so
• but	• yet	• or

   Connectives are linking words that join sentences or parts of sentences together.

3) When these words are used to <u>connect two sentences</u>, the comma shows where the <u>next point begins</u>:

   The Sun is lower in the sky, so its heat is spread over more of the Earth's surface.

   The <u>comma</u> and '<u>so</u>' join the two sentences.

   The American economy was stronger by 1935, but some problems remained.

4) <u>Longer linking words</u>, like 'however', 'therefore' and 'nevertheless',
   are also followed by a comma when they're at the <u>start</u> of a sentence:

   However, Giles Corey is one of the most likeable characters in the play.

Commas can separate information in a list and join sentences...

Using commas in lists should be quite straightforward, but using a comma to combine points is
a bit more tricky. Every time you use a connective, check whether you need a comma as well.

Commas

Commas can also be used to separate extra information in a sentence.

Commas *can also separate* Extra Information

Use a <u>pair of commas</u> to separate extra information in the <u>middle</u> of a sentence:

The animals, led by Snowball, planned a revolution.

These commas <u>enclose</u> the <u>extra information</u> — 'led by Snowball'.

The suffragists, founded in 1897, were led by Millicent Fawcett.

'<u>founded in 1897</u>' is the extra information.

Remove *the extra information to* Check *the commas are right*

You can check you've used commas <u>correctly</u> by <u>removing</u> the information <u>inside</u> the pair of commas. If the sentence still <u>makes sense</u> then you've used them right.

The Christian Holy Week which usually falls, <u>in March or April</u>, is the final week of Lent.

The commas suggest that this is <u>extra information</u>.

The Christian Holy Week which usually falls is the final week of Lent.

But if you remove the words between the commas, the sentence <u>doesn't make sense</u>. This means the commas were used <u>incorrectly</u>.

The Christian Holy Week, <u>which usually falls in March or April</u>, is the final week of Lent.

This bit is the <u>extra information</u> — if you remove it, the sentence should <u>still make sense</u>.

The Christian Holy Week is the final week of Lent.

This sentence <u>makes sense</u>, so the commas were used <u>correctly</u>.

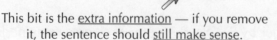

You'll probably need to use commas in your essays...

... so make sure you know how to use them properly. Too many commas and your writing won't flow; too few commas and your writing might not make sense. Keep practising until you get it right.

Commas

The **Extra Information** can also **Begin** a sentence

1) If the extra information is at the <u>beginning</u> of a sentence, you still usually need to use a <u>comma</u>.

2) In this case you only need to use a <u>single comma</u>, rather than a pair.

<u>When they had discussed the issues,</u> the leaders signed the agreement.

This is the <u>extra information</u>, so it's followed by a <u>comma</u>.

<u>Despite protests,</u> coalition forces invaded Iraq in 2003.

This is the <u>extra information</u>, because the <u>main point</u> is in the rest of the sentence.

Remove the extra info to check you're using **Commas Correctly**

You can check that you've put the comma in the right place by <u>removing</u> the extra part:

<u>Although she initially rejects him,</u> Elizabeth Bennet falls in love with Darcy.

If you <u>take away</u> the <u>extra information</u> and the sentence still makes sense, you've used the comma correctly.

Elizabeth Bennet falls in love with Darcy.

Use commas if you don't want to **Repeat** part of a sentence

When you're <u>comparing</u> two things you can use a comma to <u>avoid repeating</u> yourself:

Muslims pray in a mosque and Christians pray in a church.

The comma <u>replaces</u> the phrase '<u>pray in</u>'.

Muslims pray in a mosque and Christians, a church.

Basically, commas have a shedload of uses...

Try this exercise if you're not feeling so hot on commas. Every time you read something, try to spot the commas, then use these pages to help you decide why the author has decided to use one.

Colons and Semicolons

Colons and semicolons have several uses, for example introducing lists or joining sentences. Be careful when you use them though — getting them muddled up could lose you marks.

Colons introduce Lists

You can use a <u>colon</u> to show that what <u>follows</u> gives you <u>more information</u>. This can sometimes take the form of a <u>list</u>:

These are the main themes of the novel: loneliness, prejudice, dreams and death.

The colon goes here, just <u>before</u> the <u>information</u> about the themes.

The Earth has four basic layers: the inner core, the outer core, the mantle and the crust.

The colon goes here, <u>before</u> the <u>list</u> of layers.

Semicolons Separate things in a List

Semicolons also <u>break up</u> lists of <u>long phrases</u>:

In your introduction, outline the main argument of your essay; use separate paragraphs to explain each point clearly; in your conclusion, bring your argument together; if you have time, read your essay to check for mistakes.

You need a semicolon <u>before the 'if'</u> even though it's the last item in the list.

You <u>don't need</u> to use a <u>capital letter</u> after a <u>semicolon</u>.

The 1920s' economic boom was caused by a combination of factors. Low unemployment meant that lots of people had money to spend; low inflation meant that money wasn't losing its value as quickly as it normally would; banks were encouraged to offer cheap credit by the government; and new production methods meant goods were more affordable.

Even if the last item in the list is introduced by a <u>connective</u>, like 'and' or 'but', you <u>still</u> need a <u>semicolon</u>.

Use colons properly — don't end your essay with a :-)

Colons and semicolons aren't just for making faces in text messages — they can bag you extra SPaG marks too. Go over this page again if you need to, so you know you can definitely use them correctly.

Colons and Semicolons

Both *Colons* and *Semicolons Join* two *Sentences*

1) <u>Colons</u> join two sentences when the second sentence acts as an <u>explanation</u>:

Tropical rainforests are facing a serious problem.
<u>That problem is</u> deforestation on a large scale.

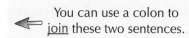

You can use a colon to
<u>join</u> these two sentences.

The colon can <u>replace this bit</u> of the sentence because
it introduces <u>further information</u> about the <u>problem</u>.

When using colons, the second sentence <u>does not</u> have to be a <u>full sentence</u>:

Tropical rainforests are facing a serious problem: deforestation on a large scale.

This colon tells you that the next
bit is going to be <u>an explanation</u>.

The bit after the colon is
<u>not a full sentence</u>.

2) <u>Semicolons</u> can join two sentences when the sentences are about the <u>same</u>
<u>thing</u>, and they have <u>equal importance</u>. Both sentences must be <u>full sentences</u>:

Orwell wrote 'Animal Farm' in 1943-44; it was difficult for him to find a publisher.

Unlike a full stop, the semicolon
shows that the <u>sentences are related</u>.

The bit <u>after the semicolon</u> could be
read as <u>a full sentence</u> on its own.

Colons and *Semicolons* are used *Differently*

Putting a <u>colon</u> or <u>semicolon</u> into a sentence can <u>change</u> its <u>meaning</u>. A colon <u>introduces</u>
<u>an explanation</u> of what comes before it, but a semicolon just <u>links</u> the <u>two sentences</u>.

George was happy; Lennie was thinking about the farm.

The semicolon shows that the
two parts are <u>related</u>, but <u>doesn't</u>
<u>explain why</u> George is happy.

George was happy: Lennie was thinking about the farm.

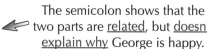

The colon shows that Lennie
'thinking about the farm' is <u>the</u>
<u>reason</u> for George's happiness.

Colons and semicolons — only impressive if used correctly...

This is pretty advanced stuff, but that doesn't mean that throwing a load of colons into your work
is going to make you look like a punctuation genius. If you're going to use them, use them right.

Brackets

Brackets are useful for adding extra information to a sentence.

Brackets enclose Extra Information in a sentence

Brackets go around <u>extra information</u> to keep it <u>separate</u>.

World War I **(**1914-1918**)** had many causes.

Brackets are always used in pairs.

This is <u>extra information</u>, so the brackets go <u>around this bit</u>.

When she learns about the prophecy **(**Act 1, Scene 5**)**, Lady Macbeth begins to plot Duncan's murder.

Brackets enclose Explanations and Definitions in a sentence

They can also separate an <u>explanation</u> or <u>definition</u>.

AIM **(**the American Indian Movement**)** was formed in 1968.

The <u>definition</u> goes <u>inside the brackets</u>.

If the information in brackets is at the <u>end</u> of the <u>sentence</u>, the full stop goes <u>outside</u> the second bracket.

In Christian teachings, marriage is for procreation **(**to have children**)**.

Brackets can be used like a pair of Commas

Brackets can be used to separate extra information in a <u>similar way</u> to a <u>pair of commas</u> (see p.38). There are a couple of things that might make you choose one piece of punctuation over the other:

<u>Commas</u> make extra information fit more <u>naturally</u> into a sentence. Brackets make it look <u>more separate</u>.

'Surrender', which is a verb, means 'to give up'.

'Surrender' (a verb) means 'to give up'.

If there are <u>already commas</u> in the main sentence or the extra information, then it's normally <u>clearer to use brackets</u>.

In this scene, Act 5, Scene 8, Macbeth is killed.

In this scene (Act 5, Scene 8) Macbeth is killed.

Don't use too many brackets...

Brackets can come in handy, but make sure you don't overuse them. Too many brackets can be a bit distracting, and there's always the danger that you may forget to close them. Nightmare.

Hyphens

Hyphens are those small dashes that join up words. Using them correctly can completely change the meaning of a word (or sentence), so they're well worth getting to grips with.

There are **Four** main places you can use a **Hyphen**

1) If the **prefix ends** with the **same letter** the **word starts with**

1) When you add a prefix which <u>ends</u> with the <u>same letter</u> that the root word <u>starts</u> with, check if you need a hyphen.

re-<u>e</u>nter   semi-<u>i</u>nterested   c<u>o</u>-operate

Prefixes are letters that go at the start of a word to change its meaning (see p.5).

2) There are <u>exceptions</u> to this rule, so make sure you learn the main ones:

mis<u>s</u>pell   un<u>n</u>ecessary   im<u>m</u>aterial   ir<u>r</u>elevant

2) If you add a **prefix** to a word starting with a **capital**

If the root word starts with a <u>capital letter</u>, use a hyphen to attach the prefix.

pro-<u>R</u>ussian   anti-<u>E</u>urope   post-<u>V</u>ictorian

3) To make the **meaning** of a **word clear**

Use a <u>hyphen</u> if the word could be <u>mixed up</u> with another word that means something <u>different</u>.

I <u>re-covered</u> the chair. ⬅ This means 'I <u>covered</u> the chair <u>again</u>'.   I <u>recovered</u> the chair. ⬅ This means 'I <u>got</u> the chair <u>back</u>'.

4) To make the **meaning** of a **phrase clear**

If it's <u>unclear</u> which word an <u>adjective applies to</u>, use a <u>hyphen</u> to make sure the meaning is clear.

new car salesman   new-<u>car</u> salesman   new <u>car-salesman</u>

The meaning of this phrase is <u>unclear</u>. You need to <u>use a hyphen</u>.

The hyphen shows that '<u>new</u>' applies to '<u>car</u>'. This means the salesman only sells <u>new cars</u>.

The hyphen shows that '<u>new</u>' applies to '<u>car salesman</u>'. This means the <u>car salesman is new</u> at his job.

I like most punctuation — but I draw the line at hyphens...

There's quite a lot to learn on this page, so go over it again if you need to. Make sure you know any words from your course that need hyphens, such as Anti-Comintern Pact, Eid al-Fitr, FARM-Africa etc.

Apostrophes

When you use a shortened form, like 'we've' instead of 'we have', you need to use an apostrophe to show that there are letters missing.

Apostrophes replace Missing Letters

Shortened words or phrases like 'you've' or 'doesn't' use apostrophes to show where letters have been removed.

Avoid using shortened forms of words like 'we're' and 'they'd' in your essays — it's better to write 'we are' or 'they had'.

We are citizens of Maycomb. We're citizens of Maycomb.

When you write 'we're' instead of 'we are', the apostrophe shows that the 'a' of 'are' has been taken out.

Atheists do not believe in God. Atheists don't believe in God.

The apostrophe shows that the 'o' in 'not' has been removed.

These forms Always have an Apostrophe

1) If any letters have been removed when a shortened word is made, you'll definitely need an apostrophe.

2) Here's a list of common ones — they're well worth learning:

Long form	Short form
I am	I'm
I would	I'd
I had	I'd
I have	I've
they are	they're

Long form	Short form
who is	who's
will not	won't
do not	don't
does not	doesn't
cannot	can't

3) It can be tricky to remember the difference between 'lets' and 'let's'.

Let's try the cabbage. 'Let's' is the shortened form of 'let us'. If the sentence makes sense with the long form then you need an apostrophe.

She lets him try it first. 'Lets' is a form of the verb 'to let'. 'She lets' means 'she allows'. 'Lets' isn't two words together so it doesn't need an apostrophe.

Apostrophes show that letters are missing...

You need to keep your wits about you with apostrophes. You definitely can't miss them out of shortened words, but make sure you don't get apostrophe happy and use them when you don't need to.

Apostrophes

As well as showing that letters are missing, apostrophes show that something belongs to someone.

Use an **Apostrophe** and **'-s'** to show **Ownership**

1) Add an <u>apostrophe</u> and '<u>-s</u>' to <u>nouns</u> to show possession:

The agency<u>'s</u> money ran out. ✓

The apostrophe shows that the money <u>belonged to</u> the agency.

The <u>agencys</u> money ran out. ✗

Without an apostrophe, the word is wrong and the sentence <u>doesn't make sense</u>.

2) You can <u>test</u> that you're using apostrophes <u>correctly</u> by <u>reordering</u> the sentence to say "the X belonging to Y".

Lennie's dream ✓ ⟹ <u>You can reorder this phrase</u> to say "the dream belonging to Lennie". The apostrophe is used <u>correctly</u>.

Three dog's ✗ ⟹ <u>If you reorder this phrase</u> to say "the three belonging to the dog" <u>it doesn't make sense</u>. This means the apostrophe is used incorrectly.

3) If the word is <u>singular</u> and <u>ends in 's'</u>, you still add an apostrophe and '-s':

Mr Jones<u>'s</u> farm is full of weeds.   The walrus<u>'s</u> food was stolen.

Add an **Apostrophe** to most **Plural Nouns** to show **Ownership**

1) If the noun is <u>plural</u> and <u>doesn't end in 's'</u>, follow the normal rule and add an <u>apostrophe and 's'</u>:

Many people feel strongly about women<u>'s</u> rights.

The rights belong to <u>more than one</u> woman, and the noun <u>doesn't end in 's'</u>, so this is the <u>correct</u> ending.

2) But if a <u>plural noun</u> already <u>ends in 's'</u>, just add an <u>apostrophe</u> to the end:

The plants<u>'</u> ecosystem   The Birlings<u>'</u> reputation

The apostrophe here shows that you're talking about <u>more than one plant</u>.

This shows that you're talking about <u>more than one member</u> of the Birling family.

Apostrophes show what belongs to whom...

Possessive apostrophes cause a lot of people bother, but just remember this golden rule. If you can reorder the sentence to say "the X belonging to Y" then you need an apostrophe. Simple as that.

Apostrophes

You can't just put apostrophes wherever you want. A badly placed apostrophe could lose you marks.

Be *Careful* when using *Apostrophes*

1) The <u>position</u> of the apostrophe is important because it can <u>change</u> the <u>meaning</u> of the sentence:

The town's buildings were devastated. ← This sentence describes what happened to the buildings of <u>one town</u>.

The towns' buildings were devastated. ← This sentence describes what happened to the buildings of <u>more than one town</u>. The <u>apostrophe's position</u> tells you whether the word is <u>singular</u> or <u>plural</u>.

2) Make sure the apostrophe goes with <u>the right word</u> in each sentence. If there are <u>two plurals</u>, it can be <u>tricky</u> to work out which word needs the apostrophe.

The governments plans ← You want this phrase to mean "<u>the plans belonging to the governments</u>".

If you're not sure which word needs a <u>plural ending</u> and which word needs a <u>possessive apostrophe</u>, reorder your sentence to say "the X belonging to Y".

The governments plan's ✗ ← If you put the apostrophe here, when you <u>reorder the phrase</u> it means "the governments belonging to the plan" which <u>doesn't make sense</u>.

The government's plans ✗ ← If you put the apostrophe here, the phrase means "the plans belonging to the government". This <u>makes sense</u>, but it's <u>not what you want to say</u>.

The governments' plans ✓ ← This means "the plans belonging to the governments" when you <u>reorder</u> it. The apostrophe is in the <u>correct place</u>.

Never use apostrophes to show there's *More Than One*

1) Because words with <u>possessive apostrophes</u> end in 's' they can easily get <u>muddled with plurals</u>.

Elizabeth and her sisters ✓

2) But you could <u>lose marks</u> if you use a possessive apostrophe with a word that is just meant to be plural.

NOT

3) If you want to say there's <u>more than one</u> of something, you usually just add an 's' on the end (see p.2-4). You <u>don't</u> need an apostrophe as well.

Elizabeth and her sister's ✗

Misplaced apostrophes are very easy for the examiner to spot...

... so it's worth learning this stuff. Taking a few seconds to think about whether you need an apostrophe is time well spent. Possessives and missing letters need apostrophes but plurals don't.

Its and It's

These words look deceptively similar, but they mean very different things...

It's means *'it is'* or *'it has'*

1) The word 'it's' <u>with an apostrophe</u> is always short for '<u>it is</u>' or '<u>it has</u>'.

2) The <u>apostrophe</u> shows that letters have been <u>missed out</u>.

<u>It is</u> caused by pollution. $\implies$ <u>It's</u> caused by pollution.

<u>It has</u> become a classic. $\implies$ <u>It's</u> become a classic.

Its shows that something **Belongs** to **It**

This is an exception to the possessive apostrophe rule on p.45.

'Its' <u>without an apostrophe</u> shows <u>possession</u> — <u>something belongs</u> to <u>it</u>.

The beast turned to show <u>its</u> face.

This shows that the face <u>belongs</u> to the beast.

The USA reduced the size of <u>its</u> navy.

This shows that the navy <u>belongs</u> to the USA.

Check that you've used *'Its'* and *'It's'* correctly

If you're <u>not sure</u> whether to use 'its' or 'it's', try <u>replacing the word</u> with 'it is' or 'it has' to see if the sentence still makes sense.

Never use <u>its'</u> — it doesn't mean anything.

Overall, <u>it's</u> been a successful project.

Check '<u>it's</u>' is right by replacing $\implies$ Overall, <u>it has</u> been a successful project. ✓
it with '<u>it is</u>' or '<u>it has</u>'.

This <u>makes sense</u>, so you know 'it's' is the <u>correct option</u> for this sentence.

<u>Its</u> windows reflected the light.

'Its' <u>doesn't need</u> an apostrophe in this sentence because it <u>can't</u> be replaced with '<u>it is</u>' or '<u>it has</u>'.

→ <u>It is</u> windows reflected the light. ✗

→ <u>It has</u> windows reflected the light. ✗

It's true — this stuff is in a league of its own...

This really has the potential to make your brain hurt. Make sure you learn the difference between these two little troublemakers so that you don't make any silly mistakes in your essays.

Speech Marks

You need to learn how to use speech marks before you can quote in your essays — that's just the way things go. This stuff isn't too scary though, so you'll get the hang of it in no time.

Speech Marks show that someone is *Speaking*

1) <u>Speech marks</u> go around the <u>actual words</u> that <u>someone says</u>.

> "What should we do about the rumours?" asked Arthur. ← This is <u>direct speech</u> — it tells you what Arthur actually said.

Speech marks go at the <u>start</u> and <u>end</u> of the speech.

2) You may need to use <u>several pairs</u> of speech marks in <u>one sentence</u>.

> "The beast had teeth," said Ralph, "and big black eyes."

The speech is <u>broken up</u> by 'said Ralph'. This means you need to use <u>two sets</u> of speech marks.

Only use **Speech Marks** for **Direct Speech**

1) You should <u>only</u> use speech marks if you quote <u>exactly</u> what someone has said (<u>direct speech</u>).

2) If you're just telling the reader <u>what someone said</u>, you <u>don't need</u> speech marks.

> Arthur asked what they should do about the rumours. ← This is called <u>indirect</u> or <u>reported speech</u> — you don't know exactly what was said.

No one is actually saying anything in this sentence, so you <u>don't need</u> any speech marks.

Speech always starts with a **Capital Letter**

1) Speech always begins with a <u>capital letter</u>, even if it starts in the <u>middle of a sentence</u>.

> Judge Taylor said, "Just tell us what happened."

2) If speech is <u>broken up</u>, the second part <u>does not need a capital</u> unless it is a new sentence.

> "He'll go to the chair," said Atticus, "unless the Governor commutes his sentence."

The <u>start</u> of the speech <u>needs a capital</u>, but <u>the second part doesn't</u>.
This is because it is <u>part of the same sentence</u> spoken by Atticus.

Let's talk about speech...

You probably won't use much direct speech in your essays, but it's best to learn the important bits, just in case. Remember that speech marks always come in pairs, so always check you've used both sets.

SECTION TWO — PUNCTUATION

Speech Marks

Speech *always ends with a* **Punctuation Mark**

1) Speech can end with a <u>comma</u>, <u>full stop</u>, <u>exclamation mark</u> or <u>question mark</u>. These usually go <u>inside</u> the speech marks.

2) If the punctuation <u>doesn't belong</u> to the <u>quotation</u>, it goes <u>outside</u> the speech marks.

He said that the play was "Shakespeare's best". ⟶ The full stop belongs to the <u>main sentence</u>, not the quotation, so it stays <u>outside the speech marks</u>.

3) Here are the <u>four main</u> pieces of punctuation that you'll come across:

1) *Most speech ends with a* **full stop**

Use a <u>full stop</u> if the sentence ends when the speech ends. ⟶ The President promised, "We'll send supplies."

A comma is needed to <u>introduce</u> the speech... ...and a full stop <u>completes</u> it.

2) *Use* **commas** *if the sentence* **isn't finished**

1) Use a <u>comma</u> if the sentence continues after the speech ends. ⟶ "Tell me more," said the Inspector.

2) If the speech is <u>split into two parts</u>, you also need a <u>comma</u>.

"Forgive them," Jesus said, "for they know not what they do."

3) *Use* **exclamation marks** *for* **strong emotions**

Use an <u>exclamation mark</u> if the speech shows strong feelings. ⟶ "Let's rebel!" shouted the animals.

The exclamation mark means you <u>don't need a comma</u> to separate the speech from the rest of the sentence.

4) *If the speech is asking a question, use a* **question mark**

Use a <u>question mark</u> if the speech is a question. ⟶ Pip asked, "What's the problem?"

Don't deliberate — punctuate...

Use the words in the sentence to help you pick the correct punctuation. 'Said' often needs a comma or a full stop; 'shouted' or 'screamed' takes an exclamation mark; and 'asked' needs a question mark.

Quoting

Quoting from texts or sources is a great way of supporting your argument, as long as you do it right.

Quoting is all about Backing Up your Points

1) Sometimes you'll need to choose a small part of a text to back up an argument or give as evidence in an essay.

2) It's best to keep your quotes short and snappy — just include the most important bits.

3) A quote on its own won't get you any marks — you need to explain why or how it supports the point you're making.

Make sure your Quotes are Accurate

1) Copy out your quotes carefully. Don't forget to use exactly the same words as the original text and copy across any punctuation or capital letters.

2) For example, you don't have to start your quote with a capital letter if it doesn't have one in the text.

> Boo is described as a monster: "he dined on raw squirrels".

Quoting from Novels or Articles

1) Quotes from any text need to be put inside speech marks. If you're just quoting a couple of words, try to include them in your sentence:

> According to the article, the rainforest is being cut down "at an alarming rate".

This quote doesn't interrupt the flow of the sentence.

2) Introduce longer quotes with a colon:

> Harper Lee compares Bob Ewell to a chicken: "a little bantam cock of a man rose and strutted to the stand".

The colon separates the quote from the rest of the sentence.

Quoting from Religious Texts

If you're taking Religious Studies, you should know how to quote from religious texts correctly. For example, if you're quoting from the Bible:

> The Bible teaches that putting wealth above God is a bad thing: "the love of money is a root of all kinds of evil" (1 Timothy 6:10).

This is the verse.

This is the book you're quoting from. This is the chapter.

If it's done right, a quote can look very impressive...

Quoting can make all the difference to your essays as long as you choose the words wisely, copy them out correctly, use the right punctuation and add a nifty explanation. Not much to remember then...

Quoting

Quoting from *Poems*

1) Write <u>short quotes</u> from poems as part of your sentence:

> In 'Quickdraw', the words "<u>trigger of my tongue</u>" sound aggressive.

2) Show where the <u>line endings</u> are for longer quotes:

The <u>colon introduces</u> the <u>quote</u>.

> 'The Farmer's Bride' uses rhyming couplets to give a song-like effect, such as:
> "We caught her, fetched her home at last **/** And turned the key upon her, fast."

Use a '/' to show where a <u>new</u> <u>line</u> in the poem begins.

3) Keep the <u>punctuation</u> the same. If the quote comes from the <u>beginning of a line</u>, it usually has a <u>capital letter</u>; if it's from the <u>end</u> of a line, you will have to include any <u>commas</u> or <u>full stops</u>.

Quoting from *Plays*

1) If you're quoting from a play which is in <u>verse</u> and your quote is <u>longer</u> than the line, you need to show where the <u>new line</u> starts.

Large parts of Shakespeare's plays are in verse.

> Capulet thinks that Juliet will be "rul'd **/** In all respects" by him.

2) If the play <u>isn't in verse</u>, you <u>don't</u> need to show the <u>line endings</u> when you quote.

> Charley gets frustrated with Willy: "When the hell are you going to grow up?"

3) If you're quoting <u>more than a couple of lines</u> or a <u>conversation</u>, you'll need to copy it out exactly as it is written in the play:

> Romeo and Juliet use religious imagery to talk about love:
>
> <u>Juliet</u>: Saints do not move, though grant for prayers' sake.
> <u>Romeo</u>: Then move not while my prayer's effect I take.
>   Thus from my lips, by thine my sin is purg'd.
>
> Act 1, Scene 5, lines 105-107

Add a little <u>explanation</u> to put the quote in <u>context</u>.

Write the <u>characters'</u> <u>names</u> here.

You need to include the <u>Act, Scene and line</u> <u>numbers</u> to show where the quote comes from.

Quoting is essential in English Literature...

You will always need to quote in your English Literature essays. When you make a point, you should use a quote or example from the text to back it up, so make sure you know how to quote properly.

Quoting

You should try to avoid really long quotes, but if you need to quote a few lines to make an important point, there is a trick to making them shorter. It could come in handy if you're caught in a tight corner...

Use **Ellipsis** to make your quotes **Shorter**

1) Sometimes you might want to use a quote that's <u>too long</u>.

   Gerald tries to excuse Sheila from the Inspector's questions: "She's had a long, exciting and tiring day <u>- we were celebrating our engagement, you know - and now</u> she's obviously had about as much as she can stand."

   This quote is <u>too long</u>. This bit <u>doesn't add anything</u>.

2) You can use an <u>ellipsis</u> (...) to cut out any part of the quote that you <u>don't need</u>.

   Gerald tries to excuse Sheila from the Inspector's questions: "She's had a long, exciting and tiring day <u>...</u> she's obviously had about as much as she can stand."

   The <u>ellipsis</u> shows that you've missed some of the quote out.

   This quote is much shorter and <u>supports the point better</u>.

You need to show **Where** the quote **Comes From**

1) You need to copy the title of the text <u>exactly</u> as it's written, and put it in <u>single speech marks</u>.

   '<u>Of Mice and Men</u>' was published in 1937.

   In '<u>The Falling Leaves</u>', the poet uses natural imagery.

2) When you're writing coursework, try to be <u>specific</u> about where in the text the quote is from.

   For novels, write the <u>chapter</u> (if the novel has chapters). ⟹ In <u>chapter 3</u>, Darcy insults Elizabeth Bennet.

   For plays, write the <u>act and scene</u>. ⟹ Lady Macbeth compares herself to men in <u>Act 1, Scene 5</u>.

Don't just make your quotes up...

In the exam you won't need to say exactly where your quotes came from, but in any coursework essays it's vital that you reference your quotes properly. Don't assume your teacher won't check.

Practice Questions

Here's another set of practice questions for you to tackle. You know the drill — answer all the questions and go over any weak spots with another round of revision.

Practice Questions

1) Rewrite these sentences, adding capital letters, full stops and question marks where they are needed.

   a)   which characters sometimes speak in latin

   b)   the boys asked whether they could play outside the school

   c)   it can be very cold in norway during december

   d)   in 1941, president roosevelt gave an important speech

2) Rewrite these sentences, adding a missing comma.

   a)   The prophets, Moses and Elijah appeared out of nowhere.

   b)   Germany, France Spain and Italy are European countries.

   c)   Unlike most authors at the time Jane Austen wrote about women.

   d)   The French Prime Minister the British Prime Minister and the President were in agreement.

   e)   The children who had studied the novel, failed to understand it.

   f)   The USA and USSR, despite their history became allies.

3) Rewrite these sentences and add a pair of brackets to each sentence.

   a)   Elizabeth I was the daughter of Henry VIII and Anne Boleyn his second wife.

   b)   Boxer a cart-horse is a determined and loyal worker on the farm.

   c)   CAFOD Catholic Agency For Overseas Development is a religious charity.

   d)   There is a consensus general agreement that glacial retreat is caused by global warming.

4) Rewrite these sentences and choose the correct form from the brackets:

   a)   Repainting the (church's/churchs') walls will cost thousands of pounds.

   b)   "(There's/Theres') nothing to worry about," said the teacher.

   c)   The (wolve's/wolves') habitat is being destroyed by urban growth.

   d)   The people in the town were impressed by the (policemen's/policemens') actions.

Exam Practice

Just when you thought you'd answered everything, there's another set of tricky questions to get your head around. Just like they say, practice makes perfect.

Practice Questions

5) Rewrite these sentences using either 'it's' or 'its':

 a) The soil had nutrients, but _____ top layer was thin.

 b) Sometimes _____ difficult to understand poetry.

 c) Look for the symbols on _____ walls.

 d) I think _____ been snowing heavily.

6) For each of these, write a short passage which includes:

 a) a short quote from a novel.

 b) a quote of more than one line from a poem.

 c) a short conversation quoted from a play.

 d) a quote from a newspaper article.

So you think you're a punctuation pro? Take a whirl at these tricky questions.
Give yourself 60 seconds to proofread each paragraph to test your punctuation prowess.

Exam Practice

1) There are 6 punctuation mistakes in the passage below. Using a pen, circle the errors and write any corrections above — give yourself 1 minute. The first one has been done for you.

In general, the higher a person's standard of living, the better their quality of life.

However a high standard of living doesnt always mean a person has a good quality of life.

For example, a person might earn lots of money, but live in a place where there's a lot of

crime and pollution. People in different part's of the world might also have different ideas

about what an acceptable quality of life is. For example, people in the UK might think it

means having a nice house owning a car and having access to leisure facilities. People in

ethiopia might think it means having clean drinking water, food and somewhere to live.

Exam Practice

Exam Practice

2) There are 6 punctuation mistakes in the passage below. Using a pen, circle the errors and write any corrections above — give yourself 1 minute. The first one has been done for you.

days

Lent commemorates the 40 days and nights Jesus spent fasting (going without food) in

the wilderness. On the day before Lent (Shrove tuesday), Roman Catholics confess their sins

and are 'shriven' (absolved from sin. Rich foods should be eaten up before the start of the

fast. For Roman Catholics, lent is traditionally a sad time where the focus of worship is on

the suffering of Jesus. Catholics, are required to abstain from meat on each Friday of Lent;

and fast for a minimum of two days.

3) There are 6 punctuation mistakes in the passage below. Using a pen, circle the errors and write any corrections above — give yourself 1 minute. The first one has been done for you.

,

In 'Of Mice and Men, John steinbeck uses Crooks to convey his ideas about race in

1930s America. Crooks is treated badly: by the other character's in a way that was typical

of the way black men were treated across America in the 1930s. While Crooks's experiences

of racial prejudice were typical of the 1930s, Steinbeck is careful not to portray Crooks in

a stereotypical way. he is presented as an intelligent character and has several books in his

room, including "a tattered dictionary.

4) There are 6 punctuation mistakes in the passage below. Using a pen, circle the errors and write any corrections above — give yourself 1 minute. The first one has been done for you.

McCarthy investigated possible communists. During hearings he intimidated witnesses

.

and pressured people to accuse others! He destroyed the careers of thousand's of people.

However, in the televised Army–McCarthy hearings (1954, his bullying turned public opinion

against him. His colleagues finally voted 67–22 to censure him in December 1954. Despite

this anti communist feeling remained strong. The Communist Control Act, for example, was

an anti-communist law that allowed dismissal from the civil service for political beliefs?

Exam Practice

Exam Practice

5) There are 6 punctuation mistakes in the passage below. Using a pen, circle the errors and write any corrections above — give yourself 1 minute. The first one has been done for you.

Tourism generates money; and is good for the economy. It creates lots of jobs for local people. Businesses that benefit include; tourist-attractions, restaurants hotels and shops. It also increases the income of other businesses that supply the tourism industry, such as the farms that supply food to hotels. Tourism is therefore important to the economy of countries in both rich and poor parts of the world. However poorer countries tend to be more dependent on the income from tourism than richer ones. For example, tourism contributes 3% of the UK's GNP and 15% of Kenya's as of 2011).

6) There are 6 punctuation mistakes in the passage below. Using a pen, circle the errors and write any corrections above — give yourself 1 minute. The first one has been done for you.

In 'An Inspector Calls', Priestley uses the reactions of the other characters to show that the Inspector's behaviour is unexpectedly blunt, and aggressive. Mr Birling accuses him of being "offensive" and tries to "protest". However, its because he says things that a normal policeman wouldnt dare to that he has power over them. Inspector Goole's repeated questions: "What was it?", "What did she say?" and "Who is to blame then!" attack the Birlings. His anger makes Mrs Birling feel "cowed and forces her to admit that she was "prejudiced against" Eva.

7) There are 6 punctuation mistakes in the passage below. Using a pen, circle the errors and write any corrections above — give yourself 1 minute. The first one has been done for you.

The Nazis took control of education and started teaching nazi propaganda. Jews were banned from teaching in schools and universities. Most teachers joined the Nazi Teachers' Association and were trained in Nazi methods Children had to report teachers who did not use them. Subjects like: history and biology were rewritten to fit in with Nazi ideas. Children were taught to be anti-Semitic, and that World War I was lost, because of jews and communists. Students in universities burned anti Nazi and Jewish books, and Jewish lecturers were sacked.

Pronouns

It's better to use pronouns in your work rather than using the same nouns over and over again. Examiners hate it when you repeat yourself. Examiners hate it when you repeat yourself. Oh...

Pronouns take the Place of Nouns

1) <u>Pronouns</u> are words that can be used instead of <u>nouns</u> so you don't keep using the <u>same words</u>.

> Napoleon changes the commandments because <u>Napoleon</u> wants to keep control.
>
> Napoleon changes the commandments because <u>he</u> wants to keep control.

'<u>He</u>' is a <u>pronoun</u> that <u>replaces</u> the <u>noun</u> 'Napoleon'.

> Macbeth and Macduff are thanes. This means <u>Macbeth</u> and <u>Macduff</u> are nobles.
>
> Macbeth and Macduff are thanes. This means <u>they</u> are nobles.

'<u>They</u>' is a <u>pronoun</u> that <u>replaces</u> the <u>nouns</u> 'Macbeth' and 'Macduff'.

2) Your writing sounds more <u>natural</u> when you use pronouns because you're not <u>repeating</u> yourself.

Pronouns Change Depending on their Function

In most passive sentences the functions of the subject and object swap over — the subject has the action done to it, and the object does the action.

1) Pronouns <u>change</u> depending on their <u>function</u> in a sentence. If the pronoun is <u>doing</u> the action it is called the <u>subject</u> of the sentence. If the pronoun is <u>receiving</u> the action it is called the <u>object</u>.

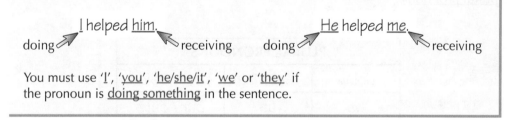

doing → <u>I</u> helped <u>him</u>. ← receiving   doing → <u>He</u> helped <u>me</u>. ← receiving

You must use '<u>I</u>', '<u>you</u>', '<u>he/she/it</u>', '<u>we</u>' or '<u>they</u>' if the pronoun is <u>doing something</u> in the sentence.

2) Pronouns can also show <u>possession</u>.

This homework is <u>mine</u>. ← This is who <u>owns</u> the <u>homework</u>.

These notes are <u>his</u>. ← This is who <u>owns</u> the <u>notes</u>.

When my teacher asked us to name two pronouns, I said "Who, me?"

You use pronouns all the time, so the stuff on this page is important. Keep in mind that pronouns will change depending on their function. Once you've understood that, you'll find pronouns a breeze.

Pronouns

There are a few more things you need to know about pronouns, as well as a couple of dos and don'ts.

Pronouns also Change Depending on the Number of People

1) Pronouns also <u>change</u> depending on <u>how many people</u> you're talking about.
2) You need to know the different <u>singular</u> and <u>plural</u> pronouns:

1) Use Singular Pronouns if you're talking about One person or thing

These are the <u>singular pronouns</u>:

SINGULAR PRONOUNS			
doing (subject)	receiving (object)	possession	
I	me	my / mine	← 1st person
you	you	your / yours	← 2nd person
he	him	his	3rd person
she	her	her / hers	
it	it	its	

The pronouns 'you' and 'it' are the same whether they're the subject or object of a sentence.

Use 'it' for things that <u>aren't people</u>.

Example: Lennie thought that <u>he</u> could look after the rabbits. ← There is <u>one person</u>, so you need a <u>singular pronoun</u>.

2) Use Plural Pronouns to talk about Two or More people or things

These are the <u>plural pronouns</u>:

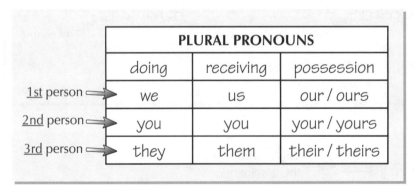

	PLURAL PRONOUNS		
	doing	receiving	possession
1st person →	we	us	our / ours
2nd person →	you	you	your / yours
3rd person →	they	them	their / theirs

Example: George and Lennie talked about <u>their</u> dream. ← There is <u>more than one person</u>, so you need a <u>plural pronoun</u>.

Use the right pronoun for the situation...

This stuff isn't too tricky to learn, so there's no excuse for getting it wrong. Use this page to refresh your knowledge, and avoid those sloppy mistakes in the exam — you don't want marks to slip away.

Pronouns

Avoid using **Too Many** *pronouns*

1) If you use <u>too many</u> pronouns it'll make your writing <u>confusing</u> for the reader.

2) Make it <u>clear</u> at the <u>start</u> of a sentence to <u>whom</u> or <u>what</u> the pronouns are <u>referring</u>:

<u>Moses</u> believed in <u>God</u> when <u>he</u> delivered <u>God's</u> message to <u>the people</u>. ✓

<u>He</u> believed in <u>him</u> when <u>he</u> delivered <u>his</u> message to <u>them</u>. ✗

This sentence uses <u>too many</u> pronouns — it's <u>not clear</u> what they all refer to.

Don't Use '**Me**' *when you mean* '**I**'

If you're writing about yourself and someone else, the other person's name always goes first — the 'I' or 'me' always comes second.

1) If a <u>pronoun</u> is <u>doing</u> the <u>action</u>, you <u>can't</u> use '<u>me</u>' — you need '<u>I</u>' instead:

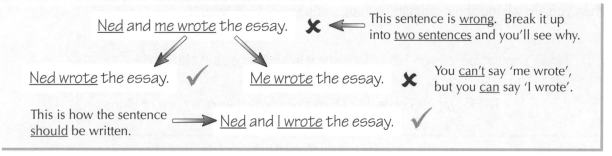

<u>Ned</u> and <u>me wrote</u> the essay. ✗ ⟵ This sentence is <u>wrong</u>. Break it up into <u>two sentences</u> and you'll see why.

<u>Ned wrote</u> the essay. ✓   <u>Me wrote</u> the essay. ✗ You <u>can't</u> say 'me wrote', but you <u>can</u> say 'I wrote'.

This is how the sentence <u>should</u> be written. ⟶ <u>Ned</u> and <u>I wrote</u> the essay. ✓

2) If a <u>pronoun</u> is <u>receiving</u> the <u>action</u> (i.e. it comes after the verb), <u>don't</u> use '<u>I</u>' — you need '<u>me</u>'.

Give the box to Kim and I. ✗   Give the box to Kim and me. ✓

<u>Remove</u> 'Kim and' from the sentence to <u>check</u> you've used the <u>correct pronoun</u>.

Give the box to I. ✗   Give the box to me. ✓

After '**Between**' *or* '**With**' *you must use* '**Me**'

A preposition is a word which tells you how things are related.

When you use <u>prepositions</u> like '<u>between</u>' or '<u>with</u>', you've got to use '<u>me</u>' rather than '<u>I</u>'.

<u>Between</u> you and <u>I</u>, this is wrong. ✗ ⟹ <u>Between</u> you and <u>me</u>, this is wrong. ✓

She came here <u>with</u> Dan and <u>I</u>. ✗ ⟹ She came here <u>with</u> Dan and <u>me</u>. ✓

Don't go over the top with pronouns...

You can't just scatter pronouns around — you've got to use them wisely or else your writing won't make a whole lot of sense. So make sure that you're very clear <u>whom</u> and <u>what</u> you're writing about.

Who, Which and That

'Who', 'which' and 'that' don't look tricky, but be warned — if used incorrectly they could be an instant SPaG mark-drainer. Read on to turn these potential mark-drainers into definite no-brainers.

Use 'Who' when you're writing about People

When you are talking about <u>people</u>, you should use '<u>who</u>'.

'That' can refer to people, but 'who' can never be used to talk about things.

> Archduke Franz Ferdinand was the man <u>who</u> was shot.
>
> It was Moses <u>who</u> led the Jews out of Egypt.

Use 'Which' when you're writing about Things

When you are talking about <u>animals</u> or <u>things</u>, you should use '<u>which</u>'.

> China's population is over 1.3 billion, <u>which</u> is the largest in the world.
>
> The Royal Air Force used Spitfires, <u>which</u> were a type of plane.

'That' is also used to write about People and Things

You can also use '<u>that</u>' to refer to either <u>things</u> or <u>people</u>, but it's better to use 'who' or 'which' <u>instead</u> of 'that' in your <u>essays</u>.

> The War of the Roses was a civil war <u>that</u> was fought in the 15th century.   This is <u>fine</u>...
>
> ... but this is <u>better</u>:   The War of the Roses was a civil war <u>which</u> was fought in the 15th century.

> It was the Prime Minister <u>that</u> was criticised.   This is <u>fine</u>...
>
> ... but this is <u>better</u>:   It was the Prime Minister <u>who</u> was criticised.

It's best to use 'who' or 'which'...

The easiest way to avoid making mistakes with this rule is to keep things simple. So you should avoid using 'that' and stick to using 'who' for writing about people, and 'which' for writing about things.

Who, Which and That

'Who', 'Which' and 'That' are used in Two main ways

1) 'Who', 'which' and 'that' crop up quite often.
2) You need to learn the main ways that you can use them:

1) You can use 'Who' and 'Which' when you ask a Question

Questions often start with 'who' or 'which':

> Who was responsible for the Cuban Missile Crisis?

'Which' can only be used for questions when there are a limited number of possible answers. Otherwise you should use 'what'.

> Which animal in the novel symbolises the working classes?

2) You can use 'Who', 'Which' and 'That' to link Two Sentences

1) 'Who', 'which' and 'that' can link two sentences together to make one sentence.
2) If you're talking about people, you should usually use 'who' or 'that'.

> Mr Birling is a character in the play. He represents the middle class.
>
> Mr Birling is a character in the play who represents the middle class.
>
> 'Who' and 'that' link the two separate sentences.
>
> Mr Birling is a character in the play that represents the middle class.

3) If you're talking about things, use 'which' or 'that'.

> Aquinas put forward an argument. It became known as the design argument.
>
> Aquinas put forward an argument which became known as the design argument.
>
> 'Which' and 'that' link the two separate sentences.
>
> Aquinas put forward an argument that became known as the design argument.

It's important to link your sentences properly...

When you're writing an essay you'll link a lot of sentences together, but it won't look great if half of those sentences are linked incorrectly. Remember, it's 'who' for people and 'which' for things.

Who or Whom, Who's or Whose

These words are all variations of 'who', so you can only use them to refer to people — simple. However, knowing when to use each one is difficult. This page should be a handy guide to put you in the know.

'Who' is the Subject of a sentence, 'Whom' is the Object

1) If the <u>person</u> you're talking about is the <u>subject</u> (doing the action) — use '<u>who</u>'.

> Seismologists are people <u>who</u> study earthquakes. ⬅ 'who' is the <u>subject</u>, '<u>earthquakes</u>' is the <u>object</u>.

2) If the <u>person</u> you're talking about is the <u>object</u> (receiving the action) — use '<u>whom</u>'.

> Eva Smith is <u>receiving</u> <u>sympathy</u> — so you need the object form '<u>whom</u>'. ⟹ Eva Smith is a character <u>whom</u> everyone can sympathise with.

3) <u>Check</u> which one to use by <u>replacing</u> 'who' or 'whom' with another <u>pronoun</u>. If a 'doing' pronoun (<u>he</u>, <u>she</u> or <u>they</u>) makes sense, use '<u>who</u>'. If a 'receiving' pronoun (<u>him</u>, <u>her</u> or <u>them</u>) works, use '<u>whom</u>'.

> Seismologists are people. <u>They</u> study earthquakes. ✓   <u>Them</u> study earthquakes. ✗
>
> Separate the sentence into <u>clauses</u>, then replace the <u>pronoun</u>. 'Seismologists' is <u>plural</u>, so you need to use '<u>they</u>' or '<u>them</u>'.   'They study earthquakes' <u>makes sense</u>, so '<u>who</u>' must be <u>right</u>.

4) With <u>trickier</u> sentences, you might need to <u>reorganise</u> the sentence when you <u>replace</u> the <u>pronoun</u>.

> Eva Smith is a character. <u>She</u> everyone can sympathise with. ⬅ This is <u>nonsense</u> — so try <u>switching</u> the order about.
>
> Everyone can sympathise with <u>she</u>. ✗   Everyone can sympathise with <u>her</u>. ✓
>
> '... sympathise with she' is <u>wrong</u> — it should be '... sympathise with her', so '<u>whom</u>' is <u>correct</u>.

'Who's' means 'Who Is' but 'Whose' is Possessive

1) '<u>Who's</u>' is the <u>shortened</u> form of '<u>who is</u>' or '<u>who has</u>'.

> <u>Who's</u> got the most lines in the play?   Romeo is the character <u>who's</u> most vocal.
>
> This means '<u>who has</u> got the most lines...'   This means '... the character <u>who is</u> most vocal.'

2) If you want to say '<u>belonging to whom</u>' you need to use '<u>whose</u>'.

> <u>Whose</u> essay is this? ⬅ This means '<u>to whom</u> does the essay belong?'

Know the difference between the subject and the object...

Lots of people don't know how to use 'whom', so they just use 'who' instead. You can stand out from the crowd by being one of the few who actually gets it right. The examiner will absolutely love that.

Verbs

Learning about verbs is as exciting as eating your greens, but it could snag you some tasty SPaG marks.

Verbs are 'Doing' or 'Being' Words

There are two types of verb — 'doing' verbs, which describe an action, and 'being' verbs, which describe a state of being.

Every sentence has to have a verb.

Dickens uses alliteration. ⟵ The verb is 'uses'.

This is a 'doing' word — 'doing' words tell you what happens.

The novel is controversial. ⟵ The verb is 'is'.

This is a 'being' word — 'being' words tell you how something is.

Verbs must always Agree with their Subjects

1) Verbs need to agree with their subject (the person or thing doing the action). If they don't agree, the sentence won't make sense.

2) Some verbs change depending on their subject. Singular subjects need a singular form of the verb, and plural subjects need a plural form of the verb.

The 'volcanologist' is the subject because he (or she) is 'doing' the action. 'Volcanologist' is singular, as it's only one person.

A volcanologist studies volcanoes.

The verb is 'studies'. It's singular.

The subject here is 'Volcanologists' — there's more than one person, so this is plural.

Volcanologists study volcanoes.

The verb 'study' is plural to match the subject.

The Tense of a verb tells you When it Happens

Verbs can be in the past tense, the present tense or the future tense.

Stalin ruled all of Russia. ⟵ past tense ⟹ Stalin has ruled all of Russia.

Stalin rules all of Russia. ⟵ present tense ⟹ Stalin is ruling all of Russia.

Stalin will rule all of Russia. ⟵ future tense ⟹ Stalin will be ruling all of Russia.

Learning about verbs makes me feel really tense...

Verbs are crucial — without them, you wouldn't have a sentence that makes any sense. What you need to know is that verbs always agree with their subject, and this can mean a change in spelling.

The Present Tense

The problem with the present tense is that people think it's easy and end up making silly mistakes. There's only one way to avoid that — you have to learn how to form it properly.

Regular Verbs follow a Pattern in the Present Tense

The <u>present</u> tense is easy to form — <u>most</u> of the <u>regular verbs</u> don't change at all. The verb only <u>changes</u> when the subject is <u>he</u>, <u>she</u> or <u>it</u>. Then you have to <u>add an '-s'</u> to the end of the verb.

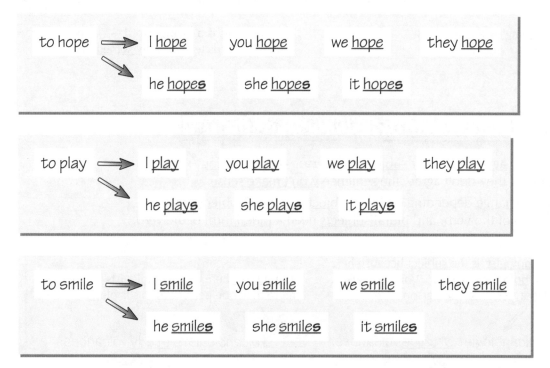

to hope ⟶ I <u>hope</u>   you <u>hope</u>   we <u>hope</u>   they <u>hope</u>
              he <u>hopes</u>   she <u>hopes</u>   it <u>hopes</u>

to play ⟶ I <u>play</u>   you <u>play</u>   we <u>play</u>   they <u>play</u>
              he <u>plays</u>   she <u>plays</u>   it <u>plays</u>

to smile ⟶ I <u>smile</u>   you <u>smile</u>   we <u>smile</u>   they <u>smile</u>
              he <u>smiles</u>   she <u>smiles</u>   it <u>smiles</u>

Watch out for Singular Nouns that refer to More than One Person

1) Some nouns like 'family', 'audience' or 'government' can be <u>singular</u> even though they refer to <u>more than one</u> person. Make sure you use the <u>third person singular</u> form of the verb.

Nouns like these can be plural if they are acting as individuals rather than as a group, e.g. 'The audience are taking their seats.'

2) The third person singular form is the form that you would use if the noun was <u>replaced</u> by the <u>pronouns</u> '<u>he</u>', '<u>she</u>' or '<u>it</u>' — you need to put an '-<u>s</u>' on the <u>end</u> of the verb.

The audience <u>stands</u> near the stage.   The family <u>travels</u> to Lisbon every year.

These words are <u>singular</u> here, so you need the <u>third person singular form</u> of the verb.

The government <u>makes</u> important decisions.   The jury <u>gives</u> its verdict.

Regular verbs in the present tense follow a simple rule...

Writing in the present tense is usually quite straightforward and, if you're careful, you won't make many mistakes using it. Just be careful with singular nouns that refer to more than one person.

The Present Tense

Well, it wasn't all going to be easy — there's a couple of trickier things you need to learn.

Learn the most common Irregular Verbs

1) A lot of verbs don't follow the regular present tense pattern — these are called irregular verbs.

2) Here are two of the most common ones. There's no trick to them — you'll just have to learn them.

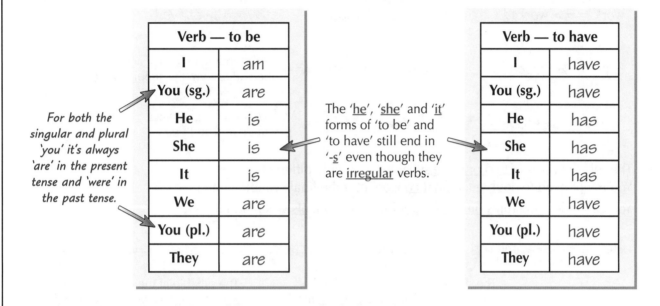

Verb — to be	
I	am
You (sg.)	are
He	is
She	is
It	is
We	are
You (pl.)	are
They	are

For both the singular and plural 'you' it's always 'are' in the present tense and 'were' in the past tense.

The 'he', 'she' and 'it' forms of 'to be' and 'to have' still end in '-s' even though they are irregular verbs.

Verb — to have	
I	have
You (sg.)	have
He	has
She	has
It	has
We	have
You (pl.)	have
They	have

For some verbs you need to Add '-es'

1) Some verbs are slightly irregular — you need to do more to them than just add '-s' when the subject is 'he', 'she' or 'it'. You need to add '-es' to these verbs:

You need to add '-es' on the end of most verbs ending in 'ss', 'x', 'sh' or 'ch'.

    it do**es**   she go**es**   he watch**es**

2) If the verb ends in a vowel or a consonant and y, you need to add '-es' to the end of the verb.

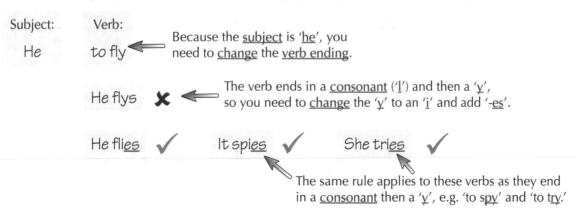

Subject: Verb:

He   to fly   Because the subject is 'he', you need to change the verb ending.

He flys   ✗   The verb ends in a consonant ('l') and then a 'y', so you need to change the 'y' to an 'i' and add '-es'.

He fli**es** ✓   It spi**es** ✓   She tri**es** ✓

The same rule applies to these verbs as they end in a consonant then a 'y', e.g. 'to spy' and 'to try.'

You've got to learn those bothersome irregular verbs...

You probably do most of this already without thinking about it too much. Still, it's pretty easy to make mistakes if you're under a lot of time pressure in an exam, so it's worth checking that this stuff's right.

The Past Tense

The past tense is like the present tense, except it talks about things that have already happened.
People are always getting past tense verbs in a tangle. You need to learn this page to stay out of trouble.

Regular Verbs add '-ed' to form the Simple Past

1) Lots of verbs form the <u>simple past</u> by <u>adding</u> '<u>-ed</u>' to the <u>end</u>.

'-ed' is a suffix, so it follows the spelling rules on p.6-7.

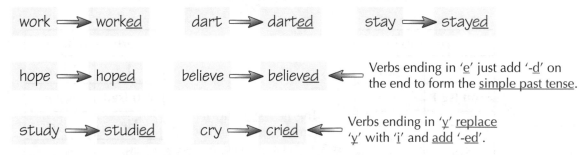

work ⟹ work<u>ed</u>   dart ⟹ dart<u>ed</u>   stay ⟹ stay<u>ed</u>

hope ⟹ hop<u>ed</u>   believe ⟹ believ<u>ed</u> ⟸ Verbs ending in '<u>e</u>' just add '<u>-d</u>' on the end to form the <u>simple past tense</u>.

study ⟹ stud<u>ied</u>   cry ⟹ cri<u>ed</u> ⟸ Verbs ending in '<u>y</u>' <u>replace</u> '<u>y</u>' with '<u>i</u>' and <u>add</u> '<u>-ed</u>'.

2) The rule for verbs of <u>two or more syllables</u> is slightly different.
You might need to <u>double</u> the <u>final consonant</u> if the final syllable is stressed.

3) You can follow the <u>rules on p.7</u> for <u>doubling consonants</u> when adding '-ed'.

admit ⟹ admitt<u>ed</u>   occur ⟹ occurr<u>ed</u>   cover ⟹ cover<u>ed</u>

The <u>stressed syllable</u> is at the end of the word, so <u>double</u> the <u>consonant</u>.

The <u>syllable</u> at the end of the word <u>isn't stressed</u>, so you just add '<u>-ed</u>'.

Irregular Verbs Don't follow the '-ed' rule

1) Not all verbs add '-ed' — lots of verbs in the simple past tense are <u>irregular</u>.

2) Here are some <u>common</u> ones:

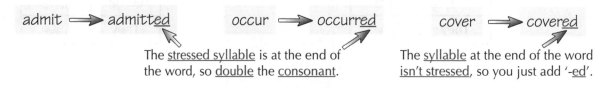

Verbs	The Simple Past
to do	did
to have	had
to see	saw
to sleep	slept
to think	thought
to make	made
to fight	fought
to come	came

Verbs	The Simple Past
to get	got
to wear	wore
to be	was / were
to go	went
to take	took
to eat	ate
to steal	stole
to buy	bought

More regular and irregular verbs — this is all very familiar...

Phew — it all seems a bit tricky. Always make sure that you've formed the past tense correctly. It's
unfortunate that lots of common words are irregular, so it's worth spending some extra time on those.

The Past Tense

Some verbs *Don't Change* to form the *Simple Past*

1) Not all verbs <u>change</u> when you form the simple past tense — some <u>stay</u> the <u>same</u>.

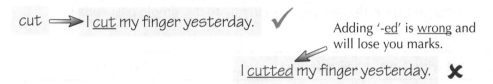

cut ⟹ I <u>cut</u> my finger yesterday. ✓

Adding '-<u>ed</u>' is <u>wrong</u> and will lose you marks.

I <u>cutted</u> my finger yesterday. ✗

2) Here are some of the most <u>common examples</u>:

| beat | cost | cut | hit | hurt | let | put | set |

The *Past Tense* with '*Have*' is *Different* from the *Simple Past*

1) The <u>past tense</u> with '<u>have</u>' describes something that happened <u>recently</u> but that has <u>finished</u> now.
2) You'll also see it used to describe something that has been <u>going on</u> for a <u>period</u> of time.

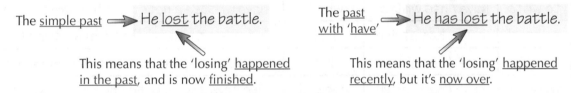

The <u>simple past</u> ⟹ He <u>lost</u> the battle.

This means that the 'losing' <u>happened</u> <u>in the past</u>, and is now <u>finished</u>.

The <u>past</u> with '<u>have</u>' ⟹ He <u>has lost</u> the battle.

This means that the 'losing' <u>happened</u> <u>recently</u>, but it's <u>now over</u>.

Learn the *Rule* for the *Past* with '*Have*'

1) The <u>past with 'have'</u> follows this <u>pattern</u>:

<u>have</u> / <u>has</u> **+** past tense with 'have' <u>verb</u>

2) Sometimes the past tense with 'have' <u>verb</u> looks the <u>same</u> as the simple past. E.g.

She <u>slept</u> well. ⟵ 'slept' looks the <u>same</u> in both tenses, but they have <u>different meanings</u>. ⟹ She <u>has slept</u> well.

3) But some past tense with 'have' <u>verbs</u> are <u>spelt differently</u> to the simple past — don't get them <u>confused</u>.

She <u>ate</u>.

She <u>has eaten</u>. ✓

She <u>has ate</u>. ✗

If you use '<u>ate</u>' when you mean '<u>eaten</u>' it'll <u>lose you marks</u>.

Check that what you've written makes sense...

Sentences in the simple past and sentences that use the past tense with 'have' might look similar, but they'll have different meanings. Reread your sentences and check what you've written makes sense.

The Past Tense

Uh-oh, here's another list of tricky words to learn. Memorise them and you'll be laughing all the way to the SPaG bank, where a big pile of lovely, golden marks await you.

You must **Learn** these **Tricky Common Verbs** with **'Have'**

Here's a list of some <u>common verbs</u> that are <u>spelt differently</u> to the <u>simple past</u> verbs:

Verbs	Past with 'have'	Simple Past	Examples
to do	have / has done	did	I have done nothing / he has done nothing
to be	have / has been	was	they have been there / she has been there
to see	have / has seen	saw	we have seen them / it has seen them
to take	have / has taken	took	you have taken over / he has taken over
to eat	have / has eaten	ate	they have eaten it / she has eaten it
to give	have / has given	gave	I have given money / he has given money
to go	have / has gone	went	you have gone to Spain / it has gone to Spain
to begin	have / has begun	began	we have begun to play / he has begun to play
to write	have / has written	wrote	I have written a note / she has written a note
to steal	have / has stolen	stole	you have stolen them / it has stolen them
to hide	have / has hidden	hid	they have hidden it / she has hidden it
to show	have / has shown	showed	we have shown faith / he has shown faith

Always write **'Done'** with **'Have'**, **'Has'** or **'Had'**

1) Never use the word '<u>done</u>' without '<u>have</u>', '<u>has</u>' or '<u>had</u>'.

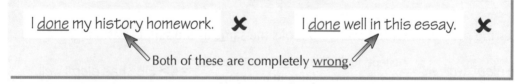

I <u>done</u> my history homework. ✖   I <u>done</u> well in this essay. ✖

Both of these are completely <u>wrong</u>.

2) You can only write '<u>I have done</u>' or '<u>I did</u>'.

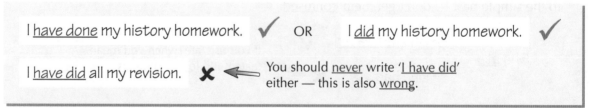

I <u>have done</u> my history homework. ✔ OR I <u>did</u> my history homework. ✔

I <u>have did</u> all my revision. ✖ ← You should <u>never</u> write '<u>I have did</u>' either — this is also <u>wrong</u>.

'Have', 'been' and 'seen' are best friends — don't split them up...

SPaG is all about getting your writing to make sense. So, when you use 'been' or 'seen' in a sentence, 'have' usually needs to make a guest appearance — otherwise your sentence won't make sense.

The Past Tense

Just a couple more things to get your head around here and then you're done with the past tense. Yay! This page is all about the dangers of using the words been and seen incorrectly.

Always use 'Been' and 'Seen' with 'Have', 'Has' or 'Had'

1) It's a common mistake to use 'been' and 'seen' without 'have', 'has' or 'had'.

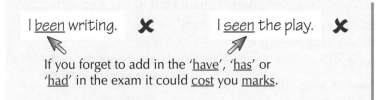

I *been* writing. ✘   I *seen* the play. ✘

If you forget to add in the 'have', 'has' or 'had' in the exam it could cost you marks.

You could also use a past tense form of the verb 'to be', if the seeing was done to them by someone else, e.g. 'They were seen by the teacher.'

2) Whenever you use 'been' or 'seen', always make sure that you have written 'have', 'has' or 'had' before it. Otherwise it's just plain wrong.

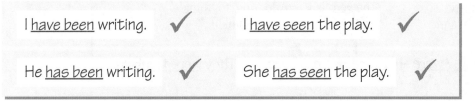

I have been writing. ✓   I have seen the play. ✓

He has been writing. ✓   She has seen the play. ✓

Don't Confuse 'Been' with 'Being' or 'Seen' with 'Seeing'

1) Even though 'been' and 'being', and 'seen' and 'seeing' sound alike, they're different tenses.

2) When you use 'been' or 'seen' you normally need to use a form of the verb 'to have'.

3) When you use 'being' or 'seeing' you need to use a form of the verb 'to be'.

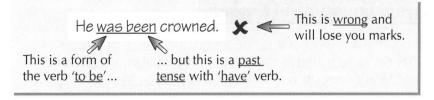

He was been crowned. ✘ ← This is wrong and will lose you marks.

This is a form of the verb 'to be'... ... but this is a past tense with 'have' verb.

4) You could either say:

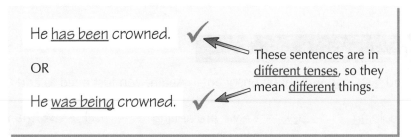

He has been crowned. ✓

OR

He was being crowned. ✓

These sentences are in different tenses, so they mean different things.

Make sure your writing isn't confusing...

Using 'been' and 'being', and 'seen' and 'seeing' correctly can be tricky because they sound similar, but make sure you pick the right one because they're totally different tenses. Don't confuse the examiner.

Forming and Spelling -ing Verbs

A really useful little grammar gem is the '-ing' form. You can use it to describe ongoing actions, either in the present or the past.

The *-ing Verb* says what *Is* or *Was Happening*

1) To talk about an <u>action</u> that <u>is still happening</u>, or <u>was still happening</u> in the past, you need to use the <u>present</u> or <u>past</u> form of the verb '<u>to be</u>' plus the <u>main verb</u> in its '<u>-ing</u>' form.

2) So, if you're writing in the present tense, you'll need either '<u>am</u>', '<u>are</u>' or '<u>is</u>'. If you're writing in the past tense, use '<u>was</u>' or '<u>were</u>'.

3) Then the <u>main verb</u> adds '<u>-ing</u>' on the end.

Main verbs are the most important verbs in a phrase.

4) Here's how to change '<u>I think</u>' into the '<u>-ing</u>' form:

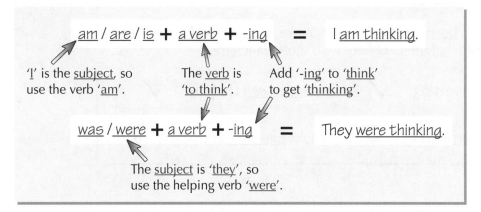

<u>am</u> / <u>are</u> / <u>is</u> **+** <u>a verb</u> **+** <u>-ing</u>   **=**   I <u>am thinking</u>.

'<u>I</u>' is the <u>subject</u>, so use the verb '<u>am</u>'.

The <u>verb</u> is '<u>to think</u>'.

Add '<u>-ing</u>' to '<u>think</u>' to get '<u>thinking</u>'.

<u>was</u> / <u>were</u> **+** <u>a verb</u> **+** <u>-ing</u>   **=**   They <u>were thinking</u>.

The <u>subject</u> is '<u>they</u>', so use the helping verb '<u>were</u>'.

Most verbs *Just Add -ing*

<u>Most verbs</u> add '<u>-ing</u>' on the end <u>without changing the spelling</u> of the verb:

1) Verbs which have a *Long Vowel Sound*

A <u>long vowel sound</u> is when a vowel has a <u>strong sound</u>, like '<u>keep</u>' or '<u>house</u>'. A long vowel often has the <u>same sound</u> as the letter of the alphabet, e.g. 'E' sounds like 'ee'. You just need to add '-ing' to verbs with <u>long vowel sounds</u>.

<u>keep</u> ⟹ he is keep<u>ing</u>   <u>eat</u> ⟹ I am eat<u>ing</u>

2) Verbs which *End* with *Two Consonants*

Verbs such as '<u>help</u>' and '<u>ask</u>' <u>end</u> with <u>two consonants</u>. Again, you just need to add '-ing'.

hel<u>p</u> ⟹ they are help<u>ing</u>   a<u>sk</u> ⟹ we are ask<u>ing</u>   fa<u>ll</u> ⟹ it is fall<u>ing</u>

How to spell -ing — a spelling problem...

A nice easy rule to learn here. Don't forget — you need to use the right form of 'to be' + verb + -ing to form this tense. You probably use '-ing' forms all the time, so you should be able to do it perfectly.

Forming and Spelling -ing Verbs

3) Some verbs which End with Two Vowels

Verbs like 'flee' and 'agree' end with two vowels. Normally you just need to add '-ing'.

flee ⟹ we are fleeing   agree ⟹ I am agreeing   see ⟹ she is seeing

You can't add '-ing' to all verbs ending in two vowels.
There are exceptions to this rule, such as words ending in '-ie':

See below for the rule for verbs ending in 'ie'.

die ⟹ dieing ✗   die ⟹ dying ✓

4) Verbs which End in 'y'

Unlike other suffixes, you don't have to worry about changing the 'y' to an 'i' when adding '-ing'. It doesn't matter if the verb ends with a consonant and then a '-y', or with a vowel and then a '-y' — you just add '-ing'.

fly ⟹ we are flying   pay ⟹ I am paying   try ⟹ she is trying

Some verbs Drop the Final 'e' before adding -ing

Verbs with a silent 'e' at the end drop the 'e' before adding '-ing'.

A silent 'e' is one which you don't hear, e.g. the 'e' at the end of 'bite'.

to take   taking

'Take' ends in a silent 'e'.   You need to remove the 'e' before adding '-ing'.

Most verbs ending in 'ie' Drop the 'e' and change the 'i' to 'y'

When you add '-ing' to most verbs ending in 'ie', such as 'tie', drop the 'e' and change the 'i' to 'y'.

tie   tying   lie   lying

'Tie' ends in 'ie'.   You need to remove the 'e' and change the 'i' to 'y' before adding '-ing'.   'Lie' ends in 'ie'.   You need to remove the 'e' and change the 'i' to 'y' before adding '-ing'.

Watch out for words where you have to remove or change letters...

Some verbs are a nightmare to spell because you have to remove or change letters. All you can do is learn the rules for spelling them and practise until you don't make any mistakes.

Forming and Spelling -ing Verbs

Here's another tricky rule to do with adding '-ing' — and of course, where there's a rule, there are exceptions to the rule. You've just got to make sure you learn them.

Some words *Double* the *Final Consonant*

1) For short verbs with <u>short vowel sounds</u> which <u>end</u> in a <u>single consonant</u> you need to <u>double the final consonant</u> (unless it's an 'x') before adding '-ing'.

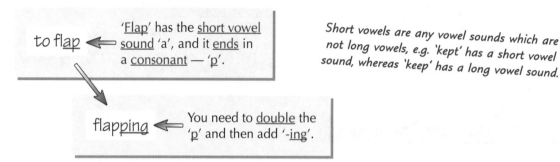

to fl<u>ap</u> ← 'Flap' has the <u>short vowel sound</u> 'a', and it <u>ends</u> in a <u>consonant</u> — 'p'.

Short vowels are any vowel sounds which are not long vowels, e.g. 'kept' has a short vowel sound, whereas 'keep' has a long vowel sound.

flap<u>ping</u> ← You need to <u>double</u> the 'p' and then add '<u>-ing</u>'.

2) Some <u>longer verbs</u> also follow this <u>pattern</u> — if the verb has <u>two</u> or <u>more syllables</u>, work out which syllable is <u>stressed</u>. A stressed syllable is the <u>part</u> of the <u>word</u> that you say with <u>more emphasis</u> (see p.7 for more on <u>stressed syllables</u>).

3) If the <u>first</u> syllable is <u>stressed</u>, just <u>add '-ing'</u>.

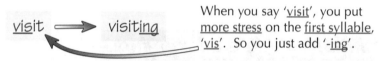

<u>visit</u> ⟹ visit<u>ing</u>

When you say '<u>visit</u>', you put <u>more stress</u> on the <u>first syllable</u>, '<u>vis</u>'. So you just add '<u>-ing</u>'.

A syllable is a word, or part of a word, which can be said in a single sound, e.g. 'beauty' has two syllables, 'beau' and 'ty'.

4) If the <u>second</u> syllable is <u>stressed</u>, <u>double</u> the <u>consonant</u> before <u>adding</u> '-ing'.

pre<u>fer</u> ⟹ prefer<u>ring</u>

When you say '<u>prefer</u>', you put <u>more stress</u> on the <u>second syllable</u>, '<u>fer</u>'. So you need to <u>double</u> the <u>final consonant</u> before adding '<u>-ing</u>'.

There are some Exceptions *to this* Rule

1) There are some <u>exceptions</u> where words <u>end</u> in an <u>unstressed syllable</u>, but the consonant is still <u>doubled</u>.

<u>wor</u>ship ⟹ worship<u>ping</u>

When you say '<u>worship</u>', you put <u>more stress</u> on the <u>first syllable</u>, '<u>wor</u>', but you still need to <u>double</u> the <u>final consonant</u> before adding '<u>-ing</u>'.

2) If a word ends in an <u>unstressed syllable</u> and then '<u>l</u>', then you need to <u>double</u> the '<u>l</u>' <u>before</u> adding '-ing'.

<u>level</u> ⟹ level<u>ling</u>

Stressed by vowels? Worry no longer...

There's an awful lot to take in on this page, so you need to read it carefully. Try your best to learn the rules. You could also make a list of useful words that double the final consonant and memorise them.

'Have' and 'Of'

One of the main mistakes with 'have' is confusing it with 'of'. Although they sound alike, they don't mean the same thing. Avoid mixing them up to get maximum SPaG marks.

It's easy to **Confuse 'Have'** and **'Of'**

1) Have a look at these <u>sentences</u>:

> They <u>could of</u> won the battle. ✗ They <u>could have</u> won the battle. ✓
>
> God <u>might of</u> made the choice. ✗ God <u>might have</u> made the choice. ✓

2) 'Could of' and 'might of' both <u>seem right</u> because they <u>sound similar</u> to the shortened versions '<u>could've</u>' and '<u>might've</u>'.

3) However, 'could of' and 'might of' are <u>wrong</u>. If you use them in the <u>exam</u> when you mean 'could have' or 'might have', you'll <u>lose marks</u>.

4) You <u>shouldn't</u> use <u>shortened versions</u> like 'could've' or 'might've' in your exam — they're <u>too informal</u>.

Use **'Have'**, NOT **'Of'**

1) It's easy to get 'could of' and 'could have' <u>muddled</u> — so, remember this golden rule. Whenever you use these <u>verbs</u>, <u>always</u> use '<u>have</u>', <u>never</u> use '<u>of</u>'.

Examiners are really picky about people writing 'of' instead of 'have'. It's worth practising this until you get it right.

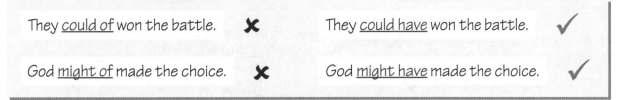

may	shall	could
might	would	can
should	will	must

2) If you're confused, remember that '<u>have</u>' is a <u>verb</u> so it follows <u>other doing words</u>, e.g.:

> ... so the rainfall <u>must have</u> been higher.   Romeo <u>could have</u> saved Juliet if he...

3) '<u>Of</u>' is a <u>preposition</u> — you'd use it in phrases such as:

> <u>Lots of</u> Muslims believe that...   Historians disagree <u>because of</u>...

All you need to remember is 'have, not of' ...

That's a useful little phrase to learn — 'have, not of'. You must remember — it doesn't matter how tempting it is to use 'of' instead of 'have', you must restrain yourself. It's always, always 'have'.

Negatives

'No' and 'not' are those great little words you use to say that you don't like something or you don't want to do something. Unfortunately, sentences with negatives like these are really easy to get wrong.

Don't use *Double Negatives*

1) <u>Double negatives</u> are when you have <u>two nos</u> or <u>nots</u> in a phrase together. It's a sure-fire way to <u>lose marks</u>, because they make your writing <u>confusing</u>.

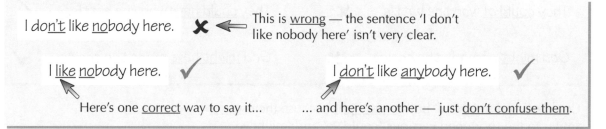

I <u>don't</u> like <u>nobody</u> here. ✗ ← This is <u>wrong</u> — the sentence 'I don't like nobody here' isn't very clear.

I <u>like</u> <u>nobody</u> here. ✓   I <u>don't</u> like <u>anybody</u> here. ✓

Here's one <u>correct</u> way to say it...   ... and here's another — just <u>don't confuse them</u>.

2) <u>Avoid</u> using the word '<u>no</u>' in phrases with '<u>-n't</u>' or '<u>not</u>'. You should use the word '<u>any</u>' instead.

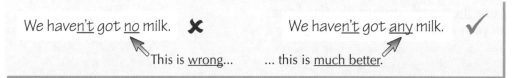

We haven't got <u>no</u> milk. ✗   We haven't got <u>any</u> milk. ✓

This is <u>wrong</u>...   ... this is <u>much better</u>.

There are *Other Words* like '*No*' you need to be careful with

1) Look out for the word '<u>no</u>' hidden in other words.

2) For example, '<u>none</u>' is <u>another word</u> like '<u>no</u>' — don't use it with another <u>negative</u>.

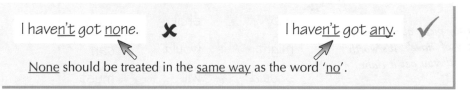

I haven't got <u>none</u>. ✗   I haven't got <u>any</u>. ✓

None should be treated in the <u>same way</u> as the word '<u>no</u>'.

3) '<u>Nothing</u>' is another example of a word like '<u>no</u>'.

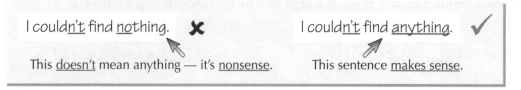

I couldn't find <u>nothing</u>. ✗   I couldn't find <u>anything</u>. ✓

This <u>doesn't</u> mean anything — it's <u>nonsense</u>.   This sentence <u>makes sense</u>.

4) '<u>Nowhere</u>' is also an example of a word like '<u>no</u>'.

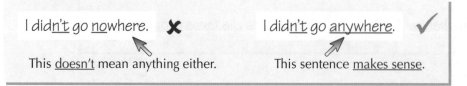

I didn't go <u>nowhere</u>. ✗   I didn't go <u>anywhere</u>. ✓

This <u>doesn't</u> mean anything either.   This sentence <u>makes sense</u>.

Two negatives are positive, but two positives aren't negative...

The mistakes on this page seem obvious when they're all laid out, but when you're in a rush and under pressure in an exam it's easy to slip up. They're the kinds of mistakes that'll cost you. So be careful.

Negatives

Watch out for words that *Seem* to be negatives, but *Aren't*

1) Words such as 'hardly', 'scarcely' and 'barely' aren't negatives, but they act in a <u>similar way</u> to negatives.

2) You <u>can't</u> use these words in a sentence <u>with</u> a negative because they <u>won't make sense</u>.

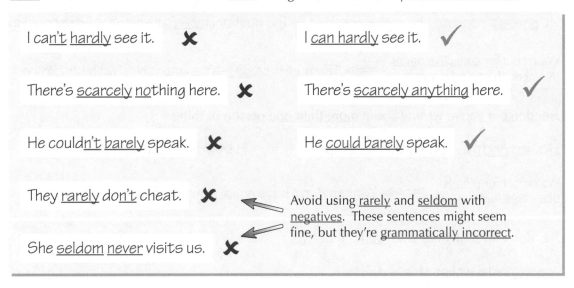

I ca<u>n't</u> <u>hardly</u> see it. ✘   I <u>can hardly</u> see it. ✔

There's <u>scarcely</u> <u>no</u>thing here. ✘   There's <u>scarcely anything</u> here. ✔

He could<u>n't</u> <u>barely</u> speak. ✘   He <u>could barely</u> speak. ✔

They <u>rarely</u> do<u>n't</u> cheat. ✘

She <u>seldom</u> <u>never</u> visits us. ✘

Avoid using <u>rarely</u> and <u>seldom</u> with <u>negatives</u>. These sentences might seem fine, but they're <u>grammatically incorrect</u>.

3) Remember, read the sentence <u>out loud</u>. If it <u>sounds wrong</u>, then it probably is wrong.

'Ain't' isn't a proper word — use 'Hasn't', 'Isn't', 'Haven't' or 'Am not'

1) Even though <u>loads</u> of people <u>use it</u>, and you might even find it in a <u>dictionary</u>, using 'ain't' in your written work is a big <u>mistake</u>.

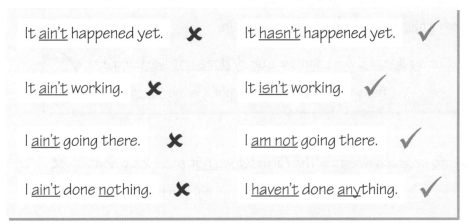

It <u>ain't</u> happened yet. ✘   It <u>hasn't</u> happened yet. ✔

It <u>ain't</u> working. ✘   It <u>isn't</u> working. ✔

I <u>ain't</u> going there. ✘   I <u>am not</u> going there. ✔

I <u>ain't</u> done <u>no</u>thing. ✘   I <u>haven't</u> done <u>any</u>thing. ✔

2) If you're not sure what to use instead of '<u>ain't</u>', try each one until one of them <u>fits</u> — you'll know when it <u>sounds right</u>.

This stuff ain't a problem...

Well, it's not a problem if you're careful with those tricky words that seem like negatives. Here's a bit of advice though: never, ever, EVER use 'ain't' in an essay. It's the most terrible of grammar crimes.

Negatives

Make sure you know the long form of each of the negatives with apostrophes — that'll help you to understand when to use them and how to use them correctly.

Don't = do not and Doesn't = does not

1) Use '<u>doesn't</u>' with '<u>he</u>', '<u>she</u>' and '<u>it</u>', or when using the name of <u>just one</u> person or thing.

> It <u>doesn't</u> support the argument.   The author <u>doesn't</u> use a lot of description.

> Watch out for <u>collective nouns</u> that need the <u>singular form</u>. The audience <u>doesn't</u> sympathise with Mr Birling.

2) Use '<u>don't</u>' if you're writing about <u>more than one</u> person or thing.

> Rivers <u>don't</u> all flow at the same speed.   Herbivores <u>don't</u> eat meat.

> Watch out for <u>plurals</u> that might look <u>singular</u>. Women <u>don't</u> have equal rights in many countries.

3) Use '<u>don't</u>' in sentences with '<u>you</u>', '<u>I</u>' or '<u>we</u>'.

> I <u>don't</u> believe that this is right.

Use the Long Form to Check you're right

If you're not sure which one is right, use the <u>long form</u> ('<u>does not</u>' or '<u>do not</u>') to check.

> Curley <u>don't</u> like Lennie = Curley <u>do not</u> like Lennie.
> This sounds <u>wrong</u> when you put it in the <u>long form</u>.

> Curley <u>doesn't</u> like Lennie = Curley <u>does not</u> like Lennie.
> This sounds <u>right</u> when you put it in the <u>long form</u>.

> The farms <u>doesn't</u> produce wheat = The farms <u>does not</u> produce wheat. ✗
> This sounds <u>wrong</u> when you put it in the <u>long form</u>.

> The farms <u>don't</u> produce wheat = The farms <u>do not</u> produce wheat.
> This sounds <u>right</u> when you put it in the <u>long form</u>.

If you're not sure, try the long form...

Working out when to use 'don't' or 'doesn't' isn't always easy. The best thing to do is check the sentence with the long form and say it out loud or in your head. You'll know which one sounds right.

Staying in the Right Tense

Switching tenses is a big mistake that you need to avoid with verbs. That means you've got to learn to use tenses properly — don't go mixing up the present with the past and the past with the future.

Don't change tenses in your writing by Mistake

Once you've picked a <u>tense</u>, you'll usually need to <u>stick to it</u>.
Make sure all the verbs <u>agree</u> with each other.

This is in the <u>past tense</u>.   Another <u>past verb</u>.

As Ralph <u>tried</u> to put the fire out, he <u>heard</u> distant splashes. Suddenly, he <u>sees</u> a boat.

This one's <u>wrong</u> — it's <u>present</u> when it should be <u>past</u>. The correct verb would be '<u>saw</u>'.

Use Past Verbs in Past Writing

1) Be consistent — <u>don't switch</u> tenses accidentally. Stay in <u>one tense</u> so it's <u>clear</u> what's going on.

2) If you <u>start</u> writing in the past, you've got to <u>stay</u> in the past.

In history essays you should usually use the past tense.

The Battle of Hastings <u>was</u> an important turning point in English history. It <u>allowed</u> William II of Normandy to seize the throne, as the English King (Harold II) <u>was killed</u> on the battlefield.

All the verbs here are <u>past forms</u> — you can tell exactly <u>what happened</u>.

Be Especially Careful with the Present

You need the <u>present</u> for <u>English literature essays</u>, but don't <u>mix</u> past and present forms by mistake.

Even though Piggy <u>is</u> annoying, Ralph <u>realised</u> he <u>is</u> his only ally. ✗

'<u>realised</u>' is <u>past tense</u>, but the rest of the sentence is in the <u>present</u>.

Even though Piggy <u>is</u> annoying, Ralph <u>realises</u> he <u>is</u> his only ally. ✓

This is how the sentence <u>should</u> be written — it's much better because the description is <u>brought to life</u> by using the <u>present</u>.

Consistency of tenses — a sticky business...

Sticking to the same tense — it sounds so simple. But when you're writing under pressure, it's easy to write the wrong thing down without thinking. Learn this page and remember your tenses when you write.

Paragraphs

Paragraphs are horrible things — you know you ought to use them, but they're a big hassle. It's really important you know how to use them so that you can improve your work.

Paragraphs make your writing Clearer

1) A paragraph is a group of sentences which talk about the same thing, or follow on from each other.

2) Every time you start a new paragraph, you're showing that something new has happened, or it's a new point.

3) Everything you write must be in paragraphs, or it could cost you — you might drop marks if you forget them.

The ideas in this paragraph are all related. They're about Boxer's injured hoof.

...but they refused to let him rest.

Boxer desperately tried to keep the pain from his split hoof hidden from the other animals. It was difficult, because he was in such agony, but he realised it was important for morale.

Benjamin knew that the pigs would never let Boxer stop work until he was physically unable to...

These paragraphs talk about something different.

Make the Beginning and End of each paragraph Clear

You need to make it clear to the examiner where each paragraph starts and finishes:

1) Leave a space on the first line.

2) Leave a gap at the end of the last sentence.

3) Start your new paragraph on a new line.

Remember the space for the next paragraph.

Start a new line and leave a gap between the margin and the first word when you begin a new paragraph.

Here's how to end a paragraph. Finish the last sentence and leave the rest of that line blank — even if there's a lot of line left.

Leave another space every time you start a new paragraph. This shows you're writing about something different.

Just leave the rest of this line blank.

No paragraphs means no more Mr Nice Examiner...

Paragraphs show the examiner when you're making a new point in your essay. If your essay is well structured, with a point per paragraph, it's easier for the examiner to give you lots of marks.

Paragraphs

There's a **Simple Trick** to **Using Paragraphs Properly**

1) Start a <u>new paragraph</u> every time something <u>changes</u> or you make a <u>new point</u>.

2) Don't worry about how <u>long</u> or <u>short</u> your <u>paragraphs</u> are — just make sure they're <u>totally clear</u>.

Use 'II' to show where a **New Paragraph Starts**

1) If you <u>forget</u> to start a new paragraph, put a <u>double strike</u> ('//') next to where your new paragraph <u>should go</u>.

For more on correcting mistakes see p.89-91.

Draw <u>two lines</u> to show where your <u>new paragraph</u> should start.

> By the end of the play, Sheila is the character who has learnt the most. She feels responsible for what she did to Eva/Daisy and tries to encourage the rest of her family to change their attitudes towards the working class.//Gerald, however, is quick to forget the Inspector's visit and thinks it has all been a "hoax"...

2) It's OK to use '//' <u>once</u> or <u>twice</u> in your essays, but don't use it all the time. It's <u>not</u> a substitute for <u>using paragraphs</u>.

When you make a **New Point**

If you're making a <u>new point</u>, you need to start a <u>new paragraph</u>.

This paragraph is about the <u>positive results</u> of <u>animal experimentation</u>.

> Some people argue that experimenting on animals is a necessary evil because it has led to the development of various vaccines and cures which have saved millions of lives.

Don't forget to leave a <u>gap</u> for <u>new paragraphs</u>.

> However, others believe that there is no justification for animal cruelty, regardless of the benefits...

This bit is arguing <u>against animal cruelty</u>, so it's a new point and needs a new paragraph.

If you've got a new point — get a new paragraph

Paragraphs aren't as pointless as you might think. Unless you write in paragraphs, it'll be difficult for the examiner to follow the thread of your answer. And that means you won't get as many SPaG marks.

Paragraphs

Remember, every time you start talking about something different, start a new paragraph.

When you talk about a **New Person**

Whenever you talk about a <u>different person</u>, you need a <u>different paragraph</u>.

This paragraph is about <u>Mrs Birling</u>.

Mrs Birling believes that reputation and social status are more important than helping people in need. She uses her "influence" to persuade members of her charity to reject Eva's desperate request for money simply because her pride has been injured.

Don't forget to leave a <u>space</u> before a new paragraph.

Gerald's a <u>new person</u>, so you need a <u>new paragraph</u>.

Gerald Croft also believes in the importance of social status and reputation, but his hypocrisy is perhaps far worse. He realises that he is acting immorally, but he still mistreats Eva, whereas Mrs Birling doesn't seem to know any better.

Mrs Birling is angrier with Eric because he recklessly risked scandal, whereas Gerald was more careful to protect his reputation.

Even if you've <u>already written</u> about these characters, you need to start a <u>new paragraph</u>.

When a new person **Speaks**

Each time a <u>new person speaks</u>, you need to start a <u>new line</u>.

Someone <u>new</u> is speaking, so you need to start a <u>new line</u>.

"The one who has dipped his hand into the bowl with me will betray me," Jesus told them.

"Surely you don't mean me, Rabbi?" replied Judas, the one who would betray him.

"You have said so," Jesus answered.

Remember to leave the rest of the line <u>blank</u> at the <u>end</u> of each paragraph.

Don't forget — a new person needs a new paragraph...

No 'ifs', 'buts' or 'maybes' — all of your essay answers should be in paragraphs. Not knowing how to use them isn't an excuse — take another look at this page and only move on when you've got it.

Paragraphs

*When you start writing about a **New Place***

A new place also needs a new paragraph.

This paragraph is about a city in Italy.

In 2009, an earthquake struck the city of L'Aquila, Italy, that measured 5.8 on the Richter scale. High standards of building construction and well-trained volunteers meant that only around 300 people died.

This needs a new paragraph, because it's talking about somewhere else.

However, in Kashmir, Pakistan, they were completely unprepared for earthquakes, which resulted in around 80 000 deaths.

It is usually the case that earthquakes which occur in more developed countries, such as Italy, have a lower death toll than earthquakes in less developed countries, such as Pakistan.

You need a new paragraph here because you are summarising what you have written above.

*When you **Move** to a **Different Time***

If you're talking about a different time, it's time for a new paragraph.

In Ancient Greece, even though medicine existed, medical knowledge was very basic. The Greeks believed that the human body contained four fluids (or humours) and that people could stay healthy by keeping the four humours in balance.

The first paragraph is about Ancient Greece.

The field of medicine had advanced significantly by the 19th century. For example, X-rays were used for the first time. These allowed doctors to see what was happening inside somebody without having to operate.

This one's gone forward to a different time — it's about the 19th century.

Nowadays medicine is advancing so quickly that it seems like anything might one day be possible. Nanorobotics and stem-cell research are just a couple of developments that could revolutionise medicine as we know it.

Finally, this paragraph has jumped forward to the present.

Different time or place = different paragraph...

Well, that's it for paragraphs. Just because these pages are at the end of the section doesn't mean that they aren't important. In fact, these pages could be some of the most important in the whole book.

Practice Questions

Think you can remember everything from the pages you've just read? Try these questions on for size....

Practice Questions

1) Rewrite these sentences by replacing the underlined words with the correct pronoun from each set of brackets.

   a) Cyclone Nargis was devastating; <u>Cyclone Nargis</u> (it/their/its) path of destruction left many people short of food.

   b) Stalin made the US go to war, which made <u>the US</u> (theirs/them/they) realise <u>Stalin</u> (him/he/his) was a threat.

   c) Catholics look to the Pope for spiritual authority; <u>Catholics</u> (we/they/you) believe <u>the Pope</u> (he/him/you) represents God.

   d) Lady Macbeth planned to kill Duncan, but <u>Lady Macbeth</u> (she/her/it) didn't kill <u>Duncan</u> (he/his/him) herself.

2) Rewrite these sentences using the correct underlined word so that they make sense.

   a) Wordsworth is one of the authors <u>whom</u>/<u>who</u> we can thank for the birth of Romanticism.

   b) There is still debate over <u>whose</u>/<u>who's</u> responsible for the assassination of President Kennedy.

   c) One campaigner <u>which</u>/<u>who</u> is very famous is Martin Luther King, <u>who's</u>/<u>whose</u> words inspired thousands.

   d) The Pope, <u>who's</u>/<u>whose</u> the leader of the Catholic Church, said <u>which</u>/<u>that</u> contraception is immoral.

3) Change the verbs in brackets so that the sentences below are in the present tense.

   a) She (to go) to every play that she can. It (to be) a time-consuming hobby, but I (to think) it's worth it.

   b) You (to try) very hard to get good marks. I (to hope) that I (to revise) enough to do just as well.

   c) My brother and I (to be) interested in physics. He often (to fly) his kite to study the effect of gravity.

   d) My teacher (to tell) us that the novel (to take) some understanding, but its message (to be) important.

4) Rewrite these phrases using the past tense with 'have'.

   a) *He begins*   c) *They do*   e) *We visit*   g) *It eats*

   b) *It hides*   d) *We have*   f) *She steals*   h) *It breaks*

Practice Questions

Practice Questions

5) Change these present tense verbs into -ing verbs.

   a) *buy*   d) *dance*   g) *dig*   j) *brake*

   b) *clap*   e) *shake*   h) *drive*   k) *win*

   c) *wait*   f) *lie*   i) *get*   l) *begin*

6) Rewrite the sentences below, correcting them as you go, so that they make perfect sense.

   a) They shouldn't of done that — it got me into trouble. I might of been given detention.

   b) You could of helped us finish dessert. We couldn't finish it because it was so sugary.

   c) The flooding may of been caused by heavy rain falling on the hills and mountains.

7) Rewrite these sentences, using either 'don't' or 'doesn't'.

   a) She _____ like me, and her brother _____ like me either.

   b) I _____ enjoy eating cabbage, but Kitty _____ enjoy eating peas.

   c) Ella and Kamal _____ have a pet, and I _____ have a bike.

   d) Frank _____ want to go to the cinema, but you _____ like going on your own.

8) Change the underlined verbs so that the tense is consistent in each sentence.

   a) When the birth rate is higher than the death rate, the population of a country <u>grew</u>.

   b) A 'holy war' <u>was</u> a war where people believe that God is 'on their side'.

   c) George <u>has decided</u> to look after Lennie because he feels sorry for him.

   d) Religion can help to bring families together, but it can also <u>caused</u> conflict.

9) Rewrite this piece of text, putting in paragraphs where you think they belong:

Hitler was able to control the lives of German people between 1933 and 1939 by using a range of methods. After 1933, all political parties other than the Nazis were banned. Communist and socialist leaders who stayed in Germany were arrested, and those who could went into exile elsewhere in Europe. The Nazis set up a series of concentration camps for all their political opponents, and these were soon used to imprison other groups in society who did not fit in with Hitler's vision of a pure German race. A system soon developed where people could be arrested and questioned without any real cause. Propaganda was also a key factor. The Party controlled all public information and nothing could be broadcast on radio, shown in cinemas or printed in newspapers unless it had been approved. The school system, youth groups and all other cultural activities were all linked to the Nazi propaganda machine.

84

Exam Practice

If you breezed through the practice questions, have a go at these tricky mixed grammar questions.

Exam Practice

1) There are 6 grammar mistakes in the passage below. Using a pen, circle the errors and write any corrections above — give yourself 1 minute. The first one has been done for you.

                                                is

'Pride and Prejudice' (was) set in Regency England when the divisions between the social classes were a lot more obvious than they were today. In the novel, Jane Austen explores the prejudices that have existed between the aristocracy, the landed gentry and the professional middle classes in the nineteenth century. This attitudes towards class and wealth are the driven force behind her characters' actions, in particular the way in which characters treat one another and which they choose to marry.

2) There are 6 grammar mistakes in the passage below. Using a pen, circle the errors and write any corrections above — give yourself 1 minute. The first one has been done for you.

                                              used

Martin Luther King and other activists (use) peaceful protests like marches, sit-ins and freedom rides who gained publicity and sympathy for the civil rights cause. Many peaceful protests was undertaken by civil rights activists: for example in 1961, CORE and the SNCC organised a series of freedom rides. Those involved groups of white Americans and African Americans sitting together on bus trips into the South. Going on freedom rides must of been terrifying because the rides were met with violence in the South, and a bus was burning in Anniston, Alabama.

3) There are 6 grammar mistakes in the passage below. Using a pen, circle the errors and write any corrections above — give yourself 1 minute. The first one has been done for you.

                        believe

Muslims (believes) that there have been many thousands of prophets in history, across all nations, revealing the nature of Allah and calling people to him. Them believe Muhammad was the final and greatest of these prophets. Muslims has special reverence for Ibrahim (Abraham), Musa (Moses) and Isa (Jesus), which are seen as deliverers of special messages from Allah, but whose messages later got add to and distorted. Other religions, such as Judaism and Christianity, also have prophets who are said to have revealed divine truths.

SEC
SEC

Exam Practice

4) There are 6 grammar mistakes in the passage below. Using a pen, circle the errors and write any corrections above — give yourself 1 minute. The first one has been done for you.

is

Subsistence farming (are) where farmers only produce enough food to feed his families.

In tropical areas farmers often clear an area of rainforest to makes land for producing food.

The soil quickly become infertile, so the farmers move to another area and start again.

These is called shifting cultivation. Subsistence farming is being replaced in some tropical

areas by commercial farming, where crops and animals is produced to be sold, e.g. coffee,

cotton, sugar cane and cattle.

5) There are 6 grammar mistakes in the passage below. Using a pen, circle the errors and write any corrections above — give yourself 1 minute. The first one has been done for you.

speaks

Friar Laurence usually (spoke) for four or five lines at once, whereas Romeo has far fewer

lines. This suggests which the Friar has more authority in the relationship. Shakespeare's use

of blank verse reinforced this portrayal of them relationship, as the Friar completes Romeo's

lines twice. This shows that Romeo hardly never gets the last word. The Friar also refers to

Romeo affectionately and informally as "pupil mine". Juliet's relationship with her Nurse is

also affectionate: the Nurse calls her "lamb" and "ladybird".

6) There are 6 grammar mistakes in the passage below. Using a pen, circle the errors and write any corrections above — give yourself 1 minute. The first one has been done for you.

that

Islam forbids using money in ways (who) might damage yourself or others; it's a basic

principle of shari'ah law. Shari'ah also forbids any financial deals involves the charging of

interest. That is to prevent rich people making more money at the expense of poorer people,

and to make sure whose wealth is spread more fairly. This means that most Muslims can't use

no Western bank accounts. Also, Muslim businesses must be ran differently from others,

because the Western economic system depends on lending money and charging interest.

Checking Your Work

Now that you've got your head around the ins and outs of SPaG, it's time to round off the fun with some exam tips. The last thing you want to do is waste your hard work by making silly mistakes on the big day.

Remember to *Check* what you've *Written*

1) Leave 5 minutes at the end of the exam to check your work.

2) Check as many questions as you can, but make sure you read over the questions which award SPaG marks especially carefully.

3) 5 minutes isn't long, so there won't be time to check everything thoroughly. Look for the most obvious spelling, punctuation and grammar mistakes.

4) Check that you've used letter combinations correctly. Follow the 'i before e' rule, check unstressed vowels and make sure that you've used double consonants where you need them.

5) Write out words and explanations in full — use 'and' instead of '&' or '+', and don't use 'etc.' when you could give more examples or a better explanation.

Watch out for *Common Spelling Errors*

Check for missing words as well as misspelt words.

When you're writing under pressure, it's easy to let spelling mistakes creep in, but there are a few things you can watch out for:

1) Look out for common homophones — words which sound the same but are spelt differently:

A glacier's size depends on <u>weather</u> it is advancing or retreating. ✗ *See p.14-23 for more on misused words.*

It's easy to get words like 'whether' and 'weather' confused, so check that you've used the right one.

A glacier's size depends on <u>whether</u> it is advancing or retreating. ✓

2) Check that you haven't used any text speak — especially shortened words:

Europe was divided <u>cos</u> of the crisis. ✗

This is text speak — it's not appropriate for the exam.

Europe was divided <u>because</u> of the crisis. ✓

3) You can impress the examiner with any technical words you've learnt for that subject, but double-check that you've spelt them all correctly (see p.27-30 for more on spelling technical words).

Checking your work in the exam is dead important...

Practise going back and checking your work when you're revising or when you're doing your homework. Then when it comes to the exam, you'll know all the things you'll need to look out for.

Checking Your Work

Don't **Repeat** yourself

Make sure you haven't <u>repeated</u> words like '<u>and</u>', '<u>but</u>' and '<u>because</u>':

> Mr Jones is lazy <u>and</u> he drinks a lot <u>and</u> he's cruel <u>and</u> selfish. ✗
>
> Using '<u>and</u>' <u>all the time</u> is really <u>boring</u>.
>
> Mr Jones is a lazy man <u>who</u> drinks a lot, <u>but</u> he's also cruel <u>and</u> selfish. ✓
>
> This is much <u>better</u> — it doesn't sound so <u>repetitive</u>.

Check for obvious **Punctuation Mistakes**

1) Make sure that every sentence <u>starts</u> with a <u>capital letter</u> and <u>ends</u> with an appropriate punctuation mark — usually a <u>full stop</u>.

2) Don't use <u>exclamation marks</u> unless they're appropriate and you're sure that you need one — chances are, you <u>won't need them</u> at all.

3) Make sure you've added <u>capital letters</u> to words that <u>always</u> need them. Here's a reminder of the most <u>common</u> ones:

See p.35 for more on capital letters.

> - people
> - towns
> - countries
> - characters
> - religions
> - titles of books, plays etc.

4) If you've <u>quoted</u> from a text, <u>check</u> the punctuation. There should be <u>speech marks</u> either side of the quote and it should have the <u>same punctuation</u> and <u>capital letters</u> as the <u>original text</u>.

> In Act 2, Scene 2, Juliet says, "Dost thou love me? I know thou wilt say 'ay'" ✗
>
> This <u>doesn't</u> have a <u>lower case letter</u> in the play, so it's <u>wrong</u>.
>
> In Act 2, Scene 2, Juliet says, "Dost thou love me? I know thou wilt say 'Ay'" ✓
>
> This is <u>better</u> — you need to <u>copy</u> the quote from the original text <u>exactly</u>.

Double-check that you've spelt your name right too...

Don't forget to factor in those crucial 5 minutes at the end of the exam to check your work — you'd be surprised how many little mistakes can slip in when you're trying to write an answer under pressure.

Checking Your Work

Grammar mistakes are easy to make, especially if you've got a brilliant idea you want to write down as quickly as possible. This page will give you a brief reminder of the most common grammatical errors.

Make sure your **Grammar** *is* **Correct**

1) Check that your writing <u>doesn't</u> sound <u>too chatty</u> — it <u>won't</u> impress the examiner.

Scout is <u>dead scared</u> of Boo Radley. ✘   Scout is <u>terrified</u> of Boo Radley. ✔

This language is <u>too informal</u> for an essay.   This language is <u>more appropriate</u>.

2) There's <u>nothing</u> more confusing than writing that <u>switches</u> between different tenses. You should usually stick to <u>just one tense</u> throughout your answer.

Most farmers <u>go</u> to market and they <u>sold</u> their goods to large chains. ✘

The first part of the sentence is in the <u>present tense</u>, so the second part should be too.

Most farmers <u>go</u> to market and they <u>sell</u> their goods to large chains. ✔

3) Check that you've started a new paragraph every time you talk about a <u>different action</u>, <u>location</u>, <u>person</u>, <u>time</u> or <u>topic</u>. It's <u>important</u> that your essay isn't just one <u>long block of text</u>.

Don't get your words **Confused**

1) Make sure that you haven't used '<u>should of</u>' when you mean '<u>should have</u>', or '<u>don't</u>' when you need '<u>doesn't</u>'.

It could <u>of</u> helped the country develop. ✘   It could <u>have</u> helped the country develop. ✔

Remember, with a verb like 'could' you <u>always</u> use '<u>have</u>', not 'of'.

It <u>don't</u> matter what I think. ✘   It <u>doesn't</u> matter what I think. ✔

Remember to use '<u>doesn't</u>' with '<u>he</u>', '<u>she</u>' or '<u>it</u>'.

2) If you know that you <u>often</u> get confused between two words, like '<u>it's</u>' and '<u>its</u>', check them <u>extra carefully</u> when you use them in the exam.

Some people argue that being virtuous is <u>it's</u> own reward. ✘

'<u>it's</u>' only has an <u>apostrophe</u> when it is a <u>shortening</u> of '<u>it has</u>' or '<u>it is</u>'.
Here it shows that the reward '<u>belongs to</u>' being virtuous, so you use '<u>its</u>'.

Some people argue that being virtuous is <u>its</u> own reward. ✔

Write a plan before you start writing your answer...

Write a plan of all the things you want to say in your answer before you start. Then you won't be worried about forgetting your ideas and you can concentrate on your SPaG while you write.

How to Correct Mistakes

So you've got 5 minutes 'til the end of the exam, the clock is ticking, and you're checking your work. Suddenly, you spot a mistake. Don't panic — you'll know what to do once you've read this stuff...

Don't Panic *if you make a* Mistake

1) <u>Don't worry</u> if you find a mistake when you <u>check</u> your work. As long as you make your corrections <u>clearly</u>, the examiner <u>won't</u> mark you down.

2) If the mistake is just <u>one word</u> or a <u>short phrase</u>, cross it out <u>neatly</u> and write the correct word <u>above</u> it.

> If a soldier was wounded, they rec<u>ie</u>ved first aid in the trench.

Here's the <u>mistake</u> you need to correct.
The '<u>ie</u>' sound does come after a '<u>c</u>', and it <u>rhymes</u> with <u>bee</u>, so it should be '<u>ei</u>'.

> received
> If a soldier was wounded, they ~~recieved~~ first aid in the trench. ✓

Draw a clear <u>line</u> through the mistake and write the whole word <u>above</u> it.

3) When you make a <u>correction</u> you need to make sure that your <u>handwriting</u> is <u>neat</u>. There's <u>no point</u> correcting a mistake if the examiner <u>can't read</u> your correction. It could mean you'll <u>miss out</u> on some <u>important marks</u>.

Make sure your Corrections *are* Neat

1) Don't write <u>on top of</u> the existing words — it's <u>much better</u> to write the new word above the old one so that the examiner can <u>read</u> your writing.

> If a soldier was wounded, they recved first aid in the trench. ✗

Your writing <u>won't be clear</u> if you write over what you've already written.

2) Don't <u>scribble out</u> a mistake — just draw a <u>line</u> through it.

> received
> If a soldier was wounded, they ~~recieved~~ first aid in the trench. ✗

It doesn't look very neat if you <u>scribble things out</u>.

3) Don't use <u>correction fluid</u> or <u>eraser pens</u> to correct your work — it'll end up looking <u>messy</u>.

> If a soldier was wounded, they recei ed first aid in the trench. ✗

It looks <u>untidy</u> when you use <u>correction fluid</u>.

Correct me if I'm wrong, but these pages seem important...

Why, yes they are — thank you ever so much for saying so. The main thing to remember is that everyone makes mistakes, but you'll do well in SPaG if you can correct your mistakes clearly and neatly.

How to Correct Mistakes

It's really annoying if you get to the end of an answer and realise you've missed something important out. That's where your helpful little friend the asterisk (*) comes in...

Use an Asterisk to add Extra Information

1) If you've <u>missed something out</u>, think about whether you have space to write the missing bit <u>above</u> the line you've already written.

2) If you <u>can</u>, write the missing bit above with a '^' to show <u>exactly where</u> it should go.

emotional
Eric and Sheila give answers to the Inspector's questions.
^

This shows that the word 'emotional' is <u>missing</u> before 'answers'.

the Great
The 1920s were a time of plenty in America before Depression.
^

Only write the <u>missing words</u> above if it's less than <u>3 or 4 words</u>.

This shows that the words 'the' and 'Great' are <u>missing</u> before 'Depression'.

3) If the bit you've missed out <u>won't</u> fit above the line, use an <u>asterisk</u> (like this *) to show the examiner <u>where</u> the missing bit should go.

4) You should write the <u>missing words</u> at the <u>end</u> of your essay or paragraph with another asterisk next to them.

Sheila is repeatedly told to leave the room by her parents. The Birlings don't think a young woman should hear this grim story.*Sheila's a young woman who thinks for herself and breaks away from her parents' traditional views.

The <u>asterisk</u> shows that something is <u>missing</u> here.

* However, Sheila stays because she feels it's her duty to find out who's responsible.

Put the asterisk next to the <u>words</u> you want to <u>add</u>.

Too many asterisks can be confusing — writing a plan might help to make sure you don't forget any important points.

Use an asterisk if you want to add something in...

If you're adding in a whole sentence, don't forget to put the asterisk at the exact place in the text where the sentence should go. That way the examiner will be able to follow your answer more easily.

How to Correct Mistakes

Use a Double Strike to show a New Paragraph

1) If you've <u>forgotten</u> to start a <u>new paragraph</u>, use a <u>double strike</u> (like this '//')
to show where the new paragraph should <u>begin</u>.

You usually show the start of a <u>paragraph</u> with a <u>new line</u> and an <u>indent</u>.

Snowball, Napoleon and Squealer are the "cleverest of the animals". Snowball uses his intelligence to try to improve life on the farm. Because the educated animals are the most powerful on Animal Farm, the fact that Snowball is willing to share his power shows how devoted he is to animal equality. // The other animals on the farm are less educated and represent the working classes of the Soviet Union. Unlike the pigs, they have no power and believe what they are told without questioning it.

Use a <u>double strike</u> to show that a <u>new paragraph</u> should start here.

2) Remember, if you're using a <u>plan</u> to help with your <u>essay</u>,
each <u>point</u> you've written down needs a <u>new paragraph</u>.

Cross Out anything you Don't want to be Marked

1) If you've written something that you <u>don't</u> want the examiner to mark, <u>cross it out neatly</u>.

2) Cross out any <u>notes</u> by the side of your answer. If you don't <u>finish</u> your answer
<u>in time</u>, don't cross out your <u>plan</u> — the examiner might look at it to see
what you were <u>going to write</u>, and possibly give you some extra marks.

3) If you decide that one of the paragraphs in the <u>middle</u>
of your answer is <u>wrong</u>, cross it out clearly so that the
examiner <u>knows</u> you don't want them to <u>mark it</u>.

Before crossing anything out, make sure you definitely don't want it marked. There's no going back once you've put a line through it.

4) If you want to <u>cross out one paragraph</u> and <u>replace</u> it with another,
use an <u>asterisk</u> and write the new paragraph at the <u>end</u> of your essay.

5) Don't <u>scribble things out</u> without thinking — it'll make your essay look <u>messy</u>.

*Try not to cross out too much stuff —
you might get marks for some of it.*

Be as neat as you can in your exam...

If the examiner can't understand what you've written, you won't get any marks for it. That's why it's really important to correct your work neatly and carefully. So no correction fluid and no scribbles.

Exam Practice

1) On the next few pages there are passages that contain a mixture of spelling, punctuation and grammar errors. Read the passages and correct the mistakes.

2) Each passage has either 6, 11 or 16 mistakes in — read the instructions for each question carefully so you know how many to look for.

3) There are passages for each of the four SPaG subjects: History, English Literature, Geography and Religious Studies. Even if you're not studying all four subjects, it's still really good practice to rewrite all the passages.

Exam Practice

1) There are **6** SPaG mistakes in the passage below. Using a pen, circle the errors and write any corrections above — give yourself 1 minute. The first one has been done for you.

> S
> For Christians, Sunday is the 'Lord's Day'. Its when they celebrate the Sabbath.
>
> Most churches have there main service on a Sunday morning. It may be structured or
>
> spontaneous, and usually includes songs Bible readings and a sermon. The exact form of
>
> worship varies between different types of church, and although Christians shares the same
>
> beleifs about the importance of the Holy Communion, the Bible, the sermon and the Holy
>
> Spirit, they have different opinions about which one matters most.

2) There are **6** SPaG mistakes in the passage below. Using a pen, circle the errors and write any corrections above — give yourself 1 minute. The first one has been done for you.

> Waves cause the most erosion at the foot of a cliff This forms a wave-cut notch. The
>
> wave-cut notch is enlarged as erosion continues. As the notch grew, the rock above them
>
> becomes unstable and eventually collapses. The colapsed material is washed away and a
>
> new wave-cut notch starts to form. This happens repeatedly, so the cliff is all ways collapsing
>
> and retreating. A wave-cut platform is left behind as the cliff retreated.

Exam Practice

Exam Practice

3) There are **6** SPaG mistakes in the passage below. Using a pen, circle the errors and write any corrections above — give yourself 1 minute. The first one has been done for you.

Atticus is a firm, but fair, father. When Jem ruins Mrs Dubose's garden, he tells him off with a voice "like the winter wind'. He then makes Jem read regularly to Mrs Dubose as an apology. He does this to teach jem a lesson about treating people farely, but also cos he wants Jem "to see what real courage is". Although Atticus is presented as a good father he is not presented as an unrealistic, perfect one.

4) There are **6** SPaG mistakes in the passage below. Using a pen, circle the errors and write any corrections above — give yourself 1 minute. The first one has been done for you.

Shabbat is the Jewish day of rest. It commemorates the seventh day of creation, when
making
God rested after ~~makeing~~ the Universe. at the Shabbat meal, plaited loafs called challot are eaten. They commemorate the double portion of manna which God provided the day b4 each Shabbat during the Exodus. Clothes are also important to Jewish people. Many Jewish men and boys wear a cap called a kippah as a sign of respect to God. They also wear tefillin during most morning prayer's. Tefillin are leather boxes worn on the upper arm and head. These remind Jews to serve God with their heads and hearts.

5) There are **6** SPaG mistakes in the passage below. Using a pen, circle the errors and write any corrections above — give yourself 1 minute. The first one has been done for you.

To gain a large empire, Germany needed to challenge Britain's naval superiority. Between 1900 & 1914, Germany attempted to double the size of it's navy. This increased tensions with Britain, which reacts by building more (and better warships of its own. Germany's ambitions also led to tensions with France. In 1905 and 1911, Germany unsuccessfully tryed to force the French to give them influence and control in Morocco.

Exam Practice

Exam Practice

6) There are **11** SPaG mistakes in the passage below. Using a pen, circle the errors and write any corrections above — give yourself 2 minutes. The first one has been done for you.

There ~~is~~ (are) several ways that trade projects and agreements help a country to develop. Fair trade schemes inprove farmer's profits because their paid a fair price for their produce. This means that farmers who join a fair trade co-operative usualy experience a significant increase in income. As the farmers earn more their quality of life improves and they can add more too the economy, so the country has more money to spend on development.

Joining international trade agreements usually has a positive affect on a country's agriculture and development.

For example, after joining the North American Free Trade Agreement (NAFTA), Mexico increased its exports to the USA. This would of had an effect on development because the amount of money Mexico made from trade increased, so more could be spend on improving people's quality of life.

7) There are **11** SPaG mistakes in the passage below. Using a pen, circle the errors and write any corrections above — give yourself 2 minutes. The first one has been done for you.

Both the ~~poem~~ (poems) 'Wind' and 'Spellbound' describe the power of a storm and its effect on the narrator. In the case of 'Wind', the storm is described as if its an enemy attacking the land and the narrator's home, whereas in 'Spellbound' the narrator is in awe of the storm, and its advance seems wild. Both poems use vivid imagery to evoke atmosphere. The imagery in 'Spellbound' is stark and straightforward, for example 'bare boughs weighed with snow", wich gives it a lonely sad atmosphere and a sense that the narrator ain't happy. The narrator is aware of the power off the storm, but is at one with nature and don't want to retreat inside like the narrator of 'Wind'. Overall, both poets feel the power of the storms there describeing, but they have different feelings about this power

Exam Practice

8) There are **11** SPaG mistakes in the passage below. Using a pen, circle the errors and write any corrections above — give yourself 2 minutes. The first one has been done for you.

A ban on producing, distributing and selling alcohol was introduced in the US in 1920.

had

Prior to the ban, temperance movements (have) campaigned for alcohol to be banned since

the 19th century. They beleived that drinking alcohol led to violence, immoral behaviour

and family brakedown. This viewpoint was shared by many people from the middle classes

They felt that alcohol was responsible for Criminal behaviour among imigrants and the

working class. Similarly, many bisnessmen thought that alcohol made workers unreliable.

Many bars closed because they could no-longer sell alcohol. However, alcohol was

still in demand, and a market opened up for the buying and, selling of illegal liquor. The

goverment's efforts to enforce the ban didnt always succeed, because many of the police

were corrupt and took bribes from criminals to turn a blind eye to the sale of alcohol.

9) There are **11** SPaG mistakes in the passage below. Using a pen, circle the errors and write any corrections above — give yourself 2 minutes. The first one has been done for you.

Some people would argue that the Big Bang theory removes the need to believe in

C

God as a 'first cause', or creator, of the Universe. Many (c)hristians do not find the sceintific

explanation of the origin of the Universe a problem. They would argue that althrough the

Universe weren't created exactly as described in the Bible, it don't mean that God was not

involved. They believe that we should look for spiritual lessons in the creation story, rather

than treating it as a scientific theory about the Universe. Alot of non-believers argue that

other scientific discoveries also make the existance of God less likely. They argue that the

argument from design, one of the strongest arguements for the existence of God, can be said

to have being disproved bye the theory of evolution.

Exam Practice

10) There are **16** SPaG mistakes in the passage below. Using a pen, circle the errors and write any corrections above — give yourself 3 minutes. The first one has been done for you.

conflict

Throughout the novel, Golding uses the ⟨conflickt⟩ between Ralph & Jack to represent the

conflict between civilisation and barbarity in mans nature. At the end, the naval officer arrive

just in time to save Ralph from Jack's barbaric "hunt", who would of undoutedly ended in his

death. Ralph is the only source of decency and reason left on the island. If he were killed, it

would show that all the boys had irreversibly dessended into savagery. However, the novel's

ending remains ambiguous. Although the boys return to civilisation, the symbolism of the

"burning wreckage of the island" shows how savage they have become. Golding is showing

that the "beast" that terorised them is actually part of human nature and they cannot escape

from them. This evil is shown through the murders of Piggy and Simon; in contrast to the

classic adventure story; good does not triumph over evil

On the surface, the last-minute rescue at the end of 'Lord of the Flies' does seem

typical of many traditional adventure stories: after they have some exciting adventures,

the main characters is rescued and return to normal life. However, on a deeper level,

Golding uses 'lord of the Flies to challinge the message of these traditional adventure

stories. The ending shows that although the boys are returning to civilisation, they might

never be the same again.

Exam Practice

11) There are **16** SPaG mistakes in the passage below. Using a pen, circle the errors and write any corrections above — give yourself 3 minutes. The first one has been done for you.

Temperate deciduous forests are forests where trees (loose) [lose] their leaves in autumn. They are located between 40° and 60° on both sides of the equator, and are mostly found in Europe, the US, China and japan. The climate in temperate deciduous forests tend to be cool-in winter (e.g. 2 °C) and warm in summer (e.g. 19 °C.) There's rainfall all year round, but the amount varys from month to month.

A temperate deciduous forest has three layers of vegetation. The top layer was made up of trees, like oak, that grow too around 30 m tall. The middle shrub layer is made up of smaller trees, like hawthorn, who are between 5 m and 20 m tall. At ground level there's and undergrowth layer made up of small plants, for example brambles and ferns. The vegetation is adapted to the climate in several ways. For example, the trees lose their leafs in autumn. This means that more water and light reaches the forest floor in the months when its harder to get water from the frozen soil and theres not much light for photosynthesis. This also allows wildflower's (such as bluebells) to grow on the forest floor in spring.

The soil in temperate deciduous forests is deep and fertile because there's a thick layer of leaf litter produced when the trees lose their leaves. This provides exellent growing conditions for all the plants in the forest, which in turn enables the forest to sustain themselves.

Exam Practice

12) There are **16** SPaG mistakes in the passage below. Using a pen, circle the errors and write any corrections above — give yourself 3 minutes. The first one has been done for you.

President Johnson, President Nixon and Rosa Parks all made significant contributions in the struggle for civil rights in the USA. The ~~too~~ *two* presidents made their mark on the civil rights movement through politics and law. Rosa Parks, on the other hand, was a ordinary woman whose actions lead to an extraordinary campain against segregation.

Rosa Parks made her mark when she refused to give up her seat on an Alabama bus to a white man, and was arrested. Her treatment led to a bus boycott. This pieceful protest resulted in a legal challenge of the law, and the Supreme Court eventually decided, that segregation laws on buses were unconstitutional.

President Johnson was in power when the Civil Rights Act of 1964 and the Voting Rights Act of 1965 were made in to laws, both of which were very important. He also introduced a preferential hiring policy that aimed to change the under-representation of African American's in employment. President Nixon also made an important contribution, since they introduced a programme which garanteed a proportion of government contracts would be awarded-to businesses owned by ethnic minoritys, a policy that was controversial at the time.

Although all three people made contributions in the civil rights struggle, I don't think that they can all be considered equaly important. I believe that Rosa Parks made the most bravest and most inspirational mark. She was a member of a disadvantaged group hersself, and made her protest at a time when the civil rights struggle was still seeing by many people as an undeserving cause.

Exam Practice

Exam Practice

13) There are **16** SPaG mistakes in the passage below. Using a pen, circle the errors and write any corrections above — give yourself 3 minutes. The first one has been done for you.

affected

For many religious people, what they eat is ~~effected~~ by their religion. Some religions have strict laws about what believers can and cannot eat. For example, Jews believe that the Kashrut (Jewish food laws) are statutes lay down by God to test Jewish obedience, and to mark they out as different from other nations. To ignore them would be ignoreing God's instructions.

Muslims believe that they must show obedience to Allah. The Qur'an says that certain foods, such as pork, isn't aloud, and since the Qur'an is the word of Allah, it would be disobedient not to follow the food laws.

Fasting is an important feature, of many religions; for example, Muslims fast during Ramadan. This is supposed to help them understand hunger and be more willing to help others. Food can also play a simbolic role in certain religious festivals, for example the Jewish Pesach (Passover) feast, wear they eat bread that don't contain yeast.

Not all religious believers restrict their diet because of their religion. Many people think that food laws laid out in religious scriptures is out of date. We shud interpret them in light of today's culture; for example, we now use diffrent farming and slaughtering methods. Others believe that its more important to look after the body that God gave us by eating a healthy diet. These days, we now more about nutrition than we done when the scriptures were written.

Answers: Sections 1-2

Section 1

Practice Questions

1. a) classes   e) churches   i) discos
   b) cities   f) claws   j) beliefs
   c) children   g) volcanoes   k) deer
   d) teeth   h) lives   l) ladies

2. a) innumerable   d) procreation   g) submarine
   b) disapprove   e) untimely   h) irrelevant
   c) unnecessary   f) immaturity

3. a) successful   d) conquered   g) beginner
   b) forgetting   e) budgeted   h) followed
   c) thoughtless   f) forgotten

4. a) government   e) species   i) subtle
   b) debt   f) could   j) deity
   c) believe   g) when   k) separately
   d) ascended   h) atheists   l) scientific

5. a) 'Romeo and Juliet' is <u>more</u> popular than 'Macbeth' in schools, maybe because the story is <u>better</u>.
   b) In Geography, the <u>best</u> way to get a <u>better</u> mark than my friends is to do the <u>most</u> studying.
   c) China has the <u>largest</u> population in the world, with <u>more</u> than 1.3 billion people.
   d) Morale was very important in the trenches — <u>happier</u> soldiers meant <u>more effective</u> offensives.

6. a) I <u>may be</u> able to help, but then again <u>maybe</u> not.
   b) Is there <u>any way</u> to drill <u>into</u> the depths of the deepest glaciers?
   c) I was <u>altogether</u> confused by her attempt to turn a rabbit <u>into</u> a dove.
   d) They came <u>in to</u> investigate <u>everybody's</u> alibis.

7. a) <u>Their</u> aim was to avoid the impact of war, but it still had an <u>effect</u> on the country.
   b) In the <u>past</u>, Jews <u>were</u> discouraged from marrying someone from another religious faith.
   c) The Inspector is a plot <u>device</u> designed to force the Birlings to <u>accept</u> their wrongdoings.
   d) It is important to <u>practise</u> emergency drills in countries <u>where</u> earthquakes are common.

8. a) It was <u>thought</u> that $30 billion was lost within <u>two</u> days as a result of the Wall Street Crash.
   b) The values in 'To Kill a Mockingbird' will <u>teach</u> you a lot because many of <u>them</u> are still relevant.
   c) <u>Our</u> research into renewable energy has been very <u>thorough</u> in the last few years.
   d) The teachings <u>of</u> Judaism and Islam are against euthanasia. Catholics are opposed <u>to</u> it <u>too</u>.

9. Answers may vary, e.g. strength = <u>S</u>ometimes <u>T</u>he <u>R</u>abid <u>E</u>lephant <u>N</u>ever <u>G</u>ets <u>T</u>o <u>H</u>ospital.

10. a) <u>misspelt</u>   e) <u>ceiling</u>   i) insightful
    b) <u>shelves</u>   f) alphabetical   j) <u>brushes</u>
    c) <u>supposed</u>   g) <u>accept</u>   k) criticism
    d) progressing   h) <u>seize</u>   l) <u>although</u>

Exam Practice

For these questions the incorrect spellings have been underlined and corrected.

1. During World War I, many women had the <u>opportunity</u> to work for the first time. Men's jobs were suddenly <u>available</u> because they were away fighting, and women were happy to take them. They wanted to prove that they <u>were</u> just as capable as men. Women worked as bus conductors and farm workers, and took <u>technical</u> jobs in engineering workshops. The women who worked in factories made <u>essential</u> goods for the war, like weapons <u>and</u> uniforms, which had a direct effect on the war effort.

2. In the UK, people are living longer because of advances in medicine and improved living <u>standards</u>. This means that the proportion of older people in the population is rising. To cope with this, the <u>government</u> is <u>gradually</u> increasing the retirement age to 68 for everyone by 2046. This means <u>a lot</u> more people will be paying taxes for longer. They are also encouraging women to go back to work after having children by giving them extra tax credits for childcare. These strategies <u>may be</u> working, but it is still <u>too</u> early to tell.

3. Abortion is when a foetus is removed from the womb before it is able to survive. Many religious <u>believers</u> think that abortion is always wrong. They believe that all life belongs to God and is <u>therefore</u> holy. Only God can choose when it starts or ends. Some religious believers think that <u>allowing</u> a woman to choose <u>whether</u> or not to have an abortion is a way <u>of</u> showing compassion. This is <u>especially</u> true if the mother was raped, is very young, or the child will have serious health problems.

4. The <u>structure</u> of 'Of Mice and Men' is <u>circular</u>. The novel begins and ends with George and Lennie in the same woodland clearing. On both <u>occasions</u>, Lennie has done something wrong and the two <u>friends</u> have been forced to run away. This leaves the reader with the <u>impression</u> that the events of the novel were inevitable and the characters were <u>helpless</u> to do anything to change them.

5. Mikhail Gorbachev brought in reforms that <u>led</u> to major changes in the USSR. Gorbachev's <u>abandoning</u> of the Brezhnev Doctrine was vital in bringing about the end of the Berlin Wall. The Brezhnev Doctrine was the guarantee that the USSR <u>would</u> <u>always</u> get involved if socialism was threatened elsewhere. <u>Scrapping</u> the doctrine made it possible for Eastern European countries to escape from USSR <u>interference</u>.

Section 2

Practice Questions

1. a) <u>W</u>hich characters sometimes speak in <u>L</u>atin<u>?</u>
   b) <u>T</u>he boys asked whether they could play outside the school<u>.</u>
   c) <u>I</u>t can be very cold in <u>N</u>orway during <u>D</u>ecember<u>.</u>
   d) <u>I</u>n 1941, <u>P</u>resident <u>R</u>oosevelt gave an important speech<u>.</u>

2. a) The prophets, Moses and Elijah<u>,</u> appeared out of nowhere.
   b) Germany, France<u>,</u> Spain and Italy are European countries.
   c) Unlike most authors at the time<u>,</u> Jane Austen wrote about women.
   d) The French Prime Minister<u>,</u> the British Prime Minister and the President were in agreement.

Answers: Sections 2-3

e) The children, who had studied the novel, failed to understand it.

f) The USA and USSR, despite their history, became allies.

3 a) Elizabeth I was the daughter of Henry VIII and Anne Boleyn (his second wife).

b) Boxer (a cart-horse) is a determined and loyal worker on the farm.

c) CAFOD (Catholic Agency For Overseas Development) is a religious charity.

d) There is a consensus (general agreement) that glacial retreat is caused by global warming.

4 a) Repainting the church's walls will cost thousands of pounds.

b) "There's nothing to worry about," said the teacher.

c) The wolves' habitat is being destroyed by urban growth.

d) The people in the town were impressed by the policemen's actions.

5 a) The soil had nutrients, but its top layer was thin.

b) Sometimes it's difficult to understand poetry.

c) Look for the symbols on its walls.

d) I think it's been snowing heavily.

6 Answers may vary, e.g. a short quote from a novel = In Chapter 1, Lennie is described as being "like a terrier" when he is holding the mouse.

Make sure you follow the rules for quoting on p.50-52.

Exam Practice

For these questions the incorrect punctuation has been underlined and corrected.

1 In general, the higher a person's standard of living, the better their quality of life. However, a high standard of living doesn't always mean a person has a good quality of life. For example, a person might earn lots of money, but live in a place where there's a lot of crime and pollution. People in different parts of the world might also have different ideas about what an acceptable quality of life is. For example, people in the UK might think it means having a nice house, owning a car and having access to leisure facilities. People in Ethiopia might think it means having clean drinking water, food and somewhere to live.

2 Lent commemorates the 40 days and nights Jesus spent fasting (going without food) in the wilderness. On the day before Lent (Shrove Tuesday), Roman Catholics confess their sins and are 'shriven' (absolved from sin). Rich foods should be eaten up before the start of the fast. For Roman Catholics, Lent is traditionally a sad time where the focus of worship is on the suffering of Jesus. Catholics are required to abstain from meat on each Friday of Lent, and fast for a minimum of two days.

3 In 'Of Mice and Men', John Steinbeck uses Crooks to convey his ideas about race in 1930s America. Crooks is treated badly by the other characters in a way that was typical of the way black men were treated across America in the 1930s. While Crooks's experiences of racial prejudice were typical of the 1930s, Steinbeck is careful not to portray Crooks in a stereotypical way. He is presented as an intelligent character and has several books in his room, including "a tattered dictionary".

4 McCarthy investigated possible communists. During hearings he intimidated witnesses and pressured people to accuse others. He destroyed the careers of thousands of people. However, in the televised Army–McCarthy hearings (1954), his bullying turned public opinion against him. His colleagues finally voted 67–22 to censure him in December 1954. Despite this, anti-communist feeling remained strong. The Communist Control Act, for example, was an anti-communist law that allowed dismissal from the civil service for political beliefs.

5 Tourism generates money and is good for the economy. It creates lots of jobs for local people. Businesses that benefit include tourist attractions, restaurants, hotels and shops. It also increases the income of other businesses that supply the tourism industry, such as farms that supply food to hotels. Tourism is therefore important to the economy of countries in both rich and poor parts of the world. However, poorer countries tend to be more dependent on the income from tourism than richer ones. For example, tourism contributes 3% of the UK's GNP and 15% of Kenya's (as of 2011).

6 In 'An Inspector Calls', Priestley uses the reactions of the other characters to show that the Inspector's behaviour is unexpectedly blunt and aggressive. Mr Birling accuses him of being "offensive" and tries to "protest". However, it's because he says things that a normal policeman wouldn't dare to that he has power over them. Inspector Goole's repeated questions: "What was it?", "What did she say?" and "Who is to blame then?" attack the Birlings. His anger makes Mrs Birling feel "cowed" and forces her to admit that she was "prejudiced against" Eva.

7 The Nazis took control of education and started teaching Nazi propaganda. Jews were banned from teaching in schools and universities. Most teachers joined the Nazi Teachers' Association and were trained in Nazi methods. Children had to report teachers who did not use them. Subjects like history and biology were rewritten to fit in with Nazi ideas. Children were taught to be anti-Semitic, and that World War I was lost because of Jews and communists. Students in universities burned anti-Nazi and Jewish books, and Jewish lecturers were sacked.

Section 3

Practice Questions

1 a) Cyclone Nargis was devastating; its path of destruction left many people short of food.

b) Stalin made the US go to war, which made them realise he was a threat.

c) Catholics look to the Pope for spiritual authority; they believe he represents God.

d) Lady Macbeth planned to kill Duncan, but she didn't kill him herself.

2 a) Wordsworth is one of the authors whom we can thank for the birth of Romanticism.

b) There is still debate over who's responsible for the assassination of President Kennedy.

c) One campaigner who is very famous is Martin Luther King, whose words inspired thousands.

d) The Pope, who's the leader of the Catholic Church, said that contraception is immoral.

Answers: Section 3

3 a) She <u>goes</u> to every play that she can. It <u>is</u> a time-consuming hobby, but I <u>think</u> it's worth it.

b) You <u>try</u> very hard to get good marks. I <u>hope</u> that I <u>revise</u> enough to do just as well.

c) My brother and I <u>are</u> interested in physics. He often <u>flies</u> his kite to study the effect of gravity.

d) My teacher <u>tells</u> us that the novel <u>takes</u> some understanding, but its message <u>is</u> important.

4 a) He has begun
b) It has hidden
c) They have done
d) We have had
e) We have visited
f) She has stolen
g) It has eaten
h) It has broken

5 a) buying
b) clapping
c) waiting
d) dancing
e) shaking
f) lying
g) digging
h) driving
i) getting
j) braking
k) winning
l) beginning

6 a) They shouldn't <u>have</u> done that — it got me into trouble. I might <u>have</u> been given detention.

b) You could <u>have</u> helped us finish dessert. We couldn't finish it because it was so sugary.

c) The flooding may <u>have</u> been caused by heavy rain falling on the hills and mountains.

7 a) She <u>doesn't</u> like me, and her brother <u>doesn't</u> like me either.

b) I <u>don't</u> enjoy eating cabbage, but Kitty <u>doesn't</u> enjoy eating peas.

c) Ella and Kamal <u>don't</u> have a pet, and I <u>don't</u> have a bike.

d) Frank <u>doesn't</u> want to go to the cinema, but you <u>don't</u> like going on your own.

8 a) When the birth rate is higher than the death rate, the population of a country <u>grows</u>.

b) A 'holy war' <u>is</u> a war where people believe that God is 'on their side'.

c) George <u>decides</u> to look after Lennie because he feels sorry for him.

d) Religion can help to bring families together, but it can also <u>cause</u> conflict.

9 Hitler was able to control the lives of German people between 1933 and 1939 by using a range of methods. After 1933, all political parties other than the Nazis were banned. Communist and socialist leaders who stayed in Germany were arrested, and those who could went into exile elsewhere in Europe.
(This paragraph is about the <u>repression of political parties</u>.)

The Nazis set up a series of concentration camps for all their political opponents, and these were soon used to imprison other groups in society who did not fit in with Hitler's vision of a pure German race. A system soon developed where people could be arrested and questioned without any real cause.
(This paragraph is about <u>concentration camps</u>.)

Propaganda was also a key factor. The Party controlled all public information and nothing could be broadcast on radio, shown in cinemas or printed in newspapers unless it had been approved. The school system, youth groups and all other cultural activities were all linked to the Nazi propaganda machine.
(This paragraph is about <u>propaganda</u>.)

Exam Practice

For these questions the incorrect grammar has been underlined and corrected.

1 'Pride and Prejudice' <u>is</u> set in Regency England when the divisions between the social classes were a lot more obvious than they <u>are</u> today. In the novel, Jane Austen explores the prejudices that <u>have</u> existed between the aristocracy, the landed gentry and the professional middle classes in the nineteenth century. <u>These</u> attitudes towards class and wealth are the <u>driving</u> force behind her characters' actions, in particular the way in which characters treat one another and <u>whom</u> they choose to marry.

2 Martin Luther King and other activists <u>used</u> peaceful protests like marches, sit-ins and freedom rides <u>which / that</u> gained publicity and sympathy for the civil rights cause. Many peaceful protests <u>were</u> undertaken by civil rights activists: for example in 1961, CORE and the SNCC organised a series of freedom rides. <u>These</u> involved groups of white Americans and African Americans sitting together on bus trips into the South. Going on freedom rides must <u>have</u> been terrifying because the rides were met with violence in the South, and a bus was <u>burned / burnt</u> in Anniston, Alabama.

3 Muslims <u>believe</u> that there have been many thousands of prophets in history, across all nations, revealing the nature of Allah and calling people to him. <u>They</u> believe Muhammad was the final and greatest of these prophets. Muslims <u>have</u> special reverence for Ibrahim (Abraham), Musa (Moses) and Isa (Jesus), <u>who</u> are seen as deliverers of special messages from Allah, but whose messages later got <u>added</u> to and distorted.
(<u>new paragraph for a new point</u>)
Other religions, such as Judaism and Christianity, also have prophets who are said to have revealed divine truths.

4 Subsistence farming <u>is</u> where farmers only produce enough food to feed <u>their</u> families. In tropical areas farmers often clear an area of rainforest to <u>make</u> land for producing food. The soil quickly <u>becomes</u> infertile, so the farmers move to another area and start again. <u>This</u> is called shifting cultivation. Subsistence farming is being replaced in some tropical areas by commercial farming, where crops and animals <u>are</u> produced to be sold, e.g. coffee, cotton, sugar cane and cattle.

5 Friar Laurence usually <u>speaks</u> for four or five lines at once, whereas Romeo has far fewer lines. This suggests <u>that</u> the Friar has more authority in the relationship. Shakespeare's use of blank verse <u>reinforces</u> this portrayal of <u>their</u> relationship, as the Friar completes Romeo's lines twice. This shows that Romeo hardly <u>ever</u> gets the last word. The Friar also refers to Romeo affectionately and informally as "pupil mine".
(<u>new paragraph for a new point</u>)
Juliet's relationship with her Nurse is also affectionate: the Nurse calls her "lamb" and "ladybird".

6 Islam forbids using money in ways <u>that</u> might damage yourself or others; it's a basic principle of shari'ah law. Shari'ah also forbids any financial deals <u>involving</u> the charging of interest. <u>This</u> is to prevent rich people making more money at the expense of poorer people, and to make

Answers: Sections 3-4

sure <u>their</u> wealth is spread more fairly. This means that most Muslims can't use <s>no</s> Western bank accounts. Also, Muslim businesses must be <u>run</u> differently from others, because the Western economic system depends on lending money and charging interest.

Section 4

Exam Practice

For these questions the incorrect SPaG has been underlined and corrected.

1   For Christians, <u>S</u>unday is the 'Lord's Day'. <u>It's / It is</u> when they celebrate the Sabbath. Most churches have <u>their</u> main service on a Sunday morning. It may be structured or spontaneous, and usually includes songs<u>,</u> Bible readings and a sermon. The exact form of worship varies between different types of church, and although Christians <u>share</u> the same <u>beliefs</u> about the importance of the Holy Communion, the Bible, the sermon and the Holy Spirit, they have different opinions about which one matters most.

2   Waves cause the most erosion at the foot of a cliff<u>.</u> This forms a wave-cut notch. The wave-cut notch is enlarged as erosion continues. As the notch <u>grows</u>, the rock above <u>it</u> becomes unstable and eventually collapses. The <u>collapsed</u> material is washed away and a new wave-cut notch starts to form. This happens repeatedly, so the cliff is <u>always</u> collapsing and retreating. A wave-cut platform is left behind as the cliff <u>retreats</u>.

3   Atticus is a firm, but fair, father. When Jem ruins Mrs Dubose<u>'s</u> garden, he tells him off with a voice "like the winter wind<u>"</u>. He then makes Jem read regularly to Mrs Dubose as an apology. He does this to teach <u>J</u>em a lesson about treating people <u>fairly</u>, but also <u>because</u> he wants Jem "to see what real courage is". Although Atticus is presented as a good father<u>,</u> he is not presented as an unrealistic, perfect one.

4   Shabbat is the Jewish day of rest. It commemorates the seventh day of creation, when God rested after <u>making</u> the Universe. <u>A</u>t the Shabbat meal, plaited <u>loaves</u> called challot are eaten. They commemorate the double portion of manna which God provided the day <u>before</u> each Shabbat during the Exodus.
<u>(new paragraph for a new point)</u>

   Clothes are also important to Jewish people. Many Jewish men and boys wear a cap called a kippah as a sign of respect to God. They also wear tefillin during most morning <u>prayers</u>. Tefillin are leather boxes worn on the upper arm and head. These remind Jews to serve God with their heads and hearts.

5   To gain a large empire, Germany needed to challenge Britain<u>'s</u> naval superiority. Between 1900 <u>and</u> 1914, Germany attempted to double the size of <u>its</u> navy. This increased tensions with Britain, which <u>reacted</u> by building more (and better<u>)</u> warships of its own. Germany's ambitions also led to tensions with France. In 1905 and 1911, Germany unsuccessfully <u>tried</u> to force the French to give them influence and control in Morocco.

6   There <u>are</u> several ways that trade projects and agreements help a country to develop. Fair trade schemes <u>improve</u> <u>farmers'</u> profits because <u>they are</u> paid a fair price for their produce. This means that farmers who join a fair trade co-operative <u>usually</u> experience a significant increase in income. As the farmers earn more<u>,</u> their quality of life improves and they can add more <u>to</u> the economy, so the country has more money to spend on development.

   Joining international trade agreements usually has a positive <u>effect</u> on a country's agriculture and development. <u>(new paragraph not needed)</u> For example, after joining the North American Free Trade Agreement (NAFTA), Mexico increased its exports to the USA. This would <u>have</u> had an effect on development because the amount of money Mexico made from trade increased, so more could be <u>spent</u> on improving people's quality of life.

7   Both the <u>poems</u> 'Wind' and 'Spellbound' describe the power of a storm and its effect on the narrator. In the case of 'Wind', the storm is described as if <u>it's</u> an enemy attacking the land and the narrator's home, whereas in 'Spellbound' the narrator is in awe of the storm, and its advance seems wild. Both poems use vivid imagery to evoke atmosphere. The imagery in 'Spellbound' is stark and straightforward, for example "<u>"</u>bare boughs weighed with snow", <u>which</u> gives it a lonely<u>,</u> sad atmosphere and a sense that the narrator <u>isn't</u> happy. The narrator is aware of the power <u>of</u> the storm, but is at one with nature and <u>doesn't</u> want to retreat inside like the narrator of 'Wind'. Overall, both poets feel the power of the storms <u>they're</u> describing, but they have different feelings about this power<u>.</u>

8   A ban on producing, distributing and selling alcohol was introduced in the US in 1920. Prior to the ban, temperance movements <u>had</u> campaigned for alcohol to be banned since the 19th century. They <u>believed</u> that drinking alcohol led to violence, immoral behaviour and family <u>breakdown</u>. This viewpoint was shared by many people from the middle classes<u>.</u> They felt that alcohol was responsible for <u>c</u>riminal behaviour among <u>immigrants</u> and the working class. Similarly, many <u>businessmen</u> thought that alcohol made workers unreliable.

   Many bars closed because they could <u>no longer</u> sell alcohol. However, alcohol was still in demand, and a market opened up for the buying and<u> </u>selling of illegal liquor. The <u>government's</u> efforts to enforce the ban <u>didn't</u> always succeed, because many of the police were corrupt and took bribes from criminals to turn a blind eye to the sale of alcohol.

9   Some people would argue that the Big Bang theory removes the need to believe in God as a 'first cause', or creator, of the Universe. Many <u>C</u>hristians do not find the <u>scientific</u> explanation of the origin of the Universe a problem. They would argue that <u>although</u> the Universe <u>wasn't</u> created exactly as described in the Bible, it <u>doesn't</u> mean that God was not involved. They believe that we should look for spiritual lessons in the creation story, rather than treating it as a scientific theory about the Universe. <u>(new paragraph for a new point)</u>

Answers: Section 4

<u>A lot</u> of non-believers argue that other scientific discoveries also make the <u>existence</u> of God less likely. They argue that the argument from design, one of the strongest <u>arguments</u> for the existence of God, can be said to have <u>been</u> disproved <u>by</u> the theory of evolution.

10   Throughout the novel, Golding uses the <u>conflict</u> between Ralph <u>and</u> Jack to represent the conflict between civilisation and barbarity in <u>man's</u> nature. At the end, the naval officer <u>arrives</u> just in time to save Ralph from Jack's barbaric "hunt", <u>which</u> would <u>have</u> <u>undoubtedly</u> ended in his death. Ralph is the only source of decency and reason left on the island. If he were killed, it would show that all the boys had irreversibly <u>descended</u> into savagery. However, the novel's ending remains ambiguous. Although the boys return to civilisation, the symbolism of the "burning wreckage of the island" shows how savage they have become. Golding is showing that the "beast" that <u>terrorised</u> them is actually part of human nature and they cannot escape from <u>it</u>. This evil is shown through the murders of Piggy and Simon; in contrast to the classic adventure story<u>,</u> good does not triumph over evil<u>.</u>

    On the surface, the last-minute rescue at the end of 'Lord of the Flies' does seem typical of many traditional adventure stories: after they have some exciting adventures, the main characters <u>are</u> rescued and return to normal life. However, on a deeper level, Golding uses 'Lord of the Flies' to <u>challenge</u> the message of these traditional adventure stories. The ending shows that although the boys are returning to civilisation, they might never be the same again.

11   Temperate deciduous forests are forests where trees <u>lose</u> their leaves in autumn. They are located between 40° and 60° on both sides of the equator, and are mostly found in Europe, the US, China and <u>Japan</u>. The climate in temperate deciduous forests <u>tends</u> to be <u>cool in</u> winter (e.g. 2 °C) and warm in summer (e.g. 19 °C)<u>.</u> There's rainfall all year round, but the amount <u>varies</u> from month to month.

    A temperate deciduous forest has three layers of vegetation. The top layer <u>is</u> made up of trees, like oak, that grow <u>to</u> around 30 m tall. The middle shrub layer is made up of smaller trees, like hawthorn, <u>which / that</u> are between 5 m and 20 m tall. At ground level there's <u>an</u> undergrowth layer made up of small plants, for example brambles and ferns. The vegetation is adapted to the climate in several ways. For example, the trees lose their <u>leaves</u> in autumn. This means that more water and light reaches the forest floor in the months when <u>it's</u> harder to get water from the frozen soil and <u>there's</u> not much light for photosynthesis. This also allows <u>wildflowers</u> (such as bluebells) to grow on the forest floor in spring.

    The soil in temperate deciduous forests is deep and fertile because there's a thick layer of leaf litter produced when the trees lose their leaves. This provides <u>excellent</u> growing conditions for all the plants in the forest, which in turn enables the forest to sustain <u>itself</u>.

12   President Johnson, President Nixon and Rosa Parks all made significant contributions in the struggle for civil rights in the USA. The <u>two</u> presidents made their mark on the civil rights movement through politics and law. Rosa Parks, on the other hand, was <u>an</u> ordinary woman whose actions <u>led</u> to an extraordinary <u>campaign</u> against segregation.

Rosa Parks made her mark when she refused to give up her seat on an Alabama bus to a white man, and was arrested. Her treatment led to a bus boycott. This <u>peaceful</u> protest resulted in a legal challenge of the law, and the Supreme Court eventually decided that segregation laws on buses were unconstitutional.

    President Johnson was in power when the Civil Rights Act of 1964 and the Voting Rights Act of 1965 were made <u>into</u> laws, both of which were very important. He also introduced a preferential hiring policy that aimed to change the under-representation of African <u>Americans</u> in employment. President Nixon also made an important contribution, since <u>he</u> introduced a programme which <u>guaranteed</u> a proportion of government contracts would be <u>awarded to</u> businesses owned by ethnic <u>minorities</u>, a policy that was controversial at the time.

    Although all three people made contributions in the civil rights struggle, I don't think that they can all be considered <u>equally</u> important. I believe that Rosa Parks made the ~~most~~ bravest and most inspirational mark. She was a member of a disadvantaged group <u>herself</u>, and made her protest at a time when the civil rights struggle was still <u>seen</u> by many people as an undeserving cause.

13   For many religious people, what they eat is <u>affected</u> by their religion. Some religions have strict laws about what believers can and cannot eat. For example, Jews believe that the Kashrut (Jewish food laws) are statutes <u>laid</u> down by God to test Jewish obedience, and to mark <u>them</u> out as different from other nations. To ignore them would be <u>ignoring / to ignore</u> God's instructions.

    Muslims believe that they must show obedience to Allah. The Qur'an says that certain foods, such as pork, <u>aren't allowed</u>, and since the Qur'an is the word of Allah, it would be disobedient not to follow the food laws.

    Fasting is an important feature of many religions; for example, Muslims fast during Ramadan. This is supposed to help them understand hunger and be more willing to help others. Food can also play a <u>symbolic</u> role in certain religious festivals, for example the Jewish Pesach (Passover) feast, <u>where</u> they eat bread that <u>doesn't</u> contain yeast.

    Not all religious believers restrict their diet because of their religion. Many people think that food laws laid out in religious scriptures <u>are</u> out of date. We <u>should</u> interpret them in light of today's culture; for example, we now use <u>different</u> farming and slaughtering methods. Others believe that <u>it's</u> more important to look after the body that God gave us by eating a healthy diet. These days, we <u>know</u> more about nutrition than we <u>did</u> when the scriptures were written.

Glossary

adjective	A word that <u>describes</u> a <u>noun</u>, e.g. "<u>beautiful</u> morning", "<u>frosty</u> lawn".
adverb	A word that <u>describes</u> a <u>verb</u>, e.g. "run <u>quickly</u>", "dance <u>happily</u>".
apostrophe	A mark (') which shows that letters are <u>missing</u>, e.g. "We have" = "<u>We've</u>". Apostrophes can also show <u>possession</u> of something, e.g. "Fred's apple".
asterisk	A mark (*) which can be used to show <u>where</u> you have written <u>extra information</u>.
comparative	A word that <u>compares</u> one thing with another, e.g. "<u>shorter</u>", "<u>worse</u>".
connective	A word that <u>joins</u> two clauses or sentences, e.g. "<u>and</u>", "<u>but</u>", "<u>therefore</u>".
consonant	Any letter which is <u>not</u> a <u>vowel</u>. The vowels are a, e, i, o and u.
ellipsis	An ellipsis (…) can be used to show that <u>part of a quote</u> is missing.
homophones	Words that <u>sound the same</u>, but mean different things, e.g. "<u>hair</u>" and "<u>hare</u>".
hyphen	A small dash (-) used to <u>join up words</u>.
infinitive verb	The most <u>basic form</u> of a verb with the word '<u>to</u>' in <u>front</u> of it, e.g. "<u>to see</u>".
irregular plural	A plural which is <u>not</u> formed using a <u>standard pattern</u>, e.g. "man" becomes "<u>men</u>".
irregular verb	A verb which is <u>not</u> formed using a <u>standard pattern</u>, e.g. "to do" becomes "<u>did</u>" in the past, and "to fight" becomes "<u>fought</u>" in the past.
long vowel sound	A vowel sound which is longer than a short vowel, e.g. the vowel sound in "sl<u>o</u>pe" is long, whereas the vowel sound in "sl<u>o</u>p" is short.
mnemonic	A <u>device</u>, e.g. a sentence or a phrase, that <u>helps</u> you <u>remember information</u>.
negative	A word like "<u>no</u>", "<u>not</u>" and "<u>nothing</u>" that <u>reverses</u> the meaning of a statement, e.g. "He is playing" becomes "He is <u>not</u> playing".
noun	A word that <u>names</u> something, e.g. "<u>Paul</u>", "<u>scissors</u>", "<u>flock</u>", "<u>loyalty</u>".
object	The part of a sentence that the <u>verb</u> is being <u>done to</u>, e.g. "Tim kicked <u>the ball</u>" or "The wind howled through <u>the trees</u>".

Glossary

paragraph	A group of sentences which talk about the same thing or follow on from each other.
plural	A type of noun that tells you there is more than one of something, e.g. "rocks".
prefix	Letters that can be put in front of a word to change its meaning, e.g. "unlock".
preposition	A word that tells you how things are related, e.g. "in", "above", "before".
pronoun	A word that can be used instead of a noun, e.g. "I", "you", "he", "it".
regular plural	A plural which follows a standard pattern, e.g. add 's' to "cat" to make the plural, "cats".
regular verb	A verb which is formed using a standard pattern, e.g. adding the simple past tense ending "-ed" — "play" becomes "played" in the past.
root word	A basic word that a prefix or suffix is added to, e.g. "careless".
short vowel sound	A vowel sound which is shorter than a long vowel, e.g. the vowel sound in "kept" is short, whereas the vowel sound in "keep" is long.
silent letters	Letters that you don't hear when a word is said aloud, e.g. "gnome" or "listen".
stressed syllable	The part of a word that you say with more emphasis, e.g. "visit".
subject	The part of a sentence that the verb agrees with. It's usually the person or thing doing the action of a verb, e.g. "Jo laughed", "the bird flew".
suffix	Letters that can be put after a word to change its meaning, e.g. "playful".
superlative	A word that refers to the most or least of a group of things, e.g. "the best team".
syllable	A word, or part of a word, which can be said in a single sound, e.g. "beautiful" has three syllables, "beau-ti-ful".
tense	A verb's tense tells you whether something is in the past, present or future, e.g. "I have had a bath" = past tense, "I am having a bath" = present tense, "I will have a bath" = future tense.
unstressed vowel	Any vowel sound in a word which isn't clear when you say it aloud, e.g. "separate", "general" or "different".
verb	An action or being word, e.g. "I run", "he went", "you are".

Index